'Your body belongs to the nation'

&

other public health lobby errors

Gary Johns

Connor Court Publishing

Published in 2017 by Connor Court Publishing

Connor Court Publishing Pty Ltd.
PO Box 7257
Redland Bay QLD 4165
sales@connorcourt.com
www.connorcourt.com

Phone 0497 900 685

ISBN: 978-1-925501-49-0

Cover design, Maria Giordano

Printed in Australia

Acknowledgements

Thanks to those who have read the manuscript and made suggestions and corrections – Christopher Snowdon of the Institute of Economic Affairs, London, Nick Cater of the Menzies Research Centre, Canberra, and Professor Sinclair Davidson of RMIT, Melbourne.

Financial support for the research was provided by PMI Australia, whom I approached. The research and writing were entirely in my control at all times.

Thanks, once again, to John Nethercote, Australian Catholic University, Canberra, for his editorial skills and to Dr. Anthony Cappello and his team at Connor Court, Brisbane, for their dedication.

I am also very grateful for the support of the Business School at QUT, Brisbane, where, as a visiting fellow, I have been given generous access to the academic literature via electronic databases. These make research so much easier than was once the case.

Any errors and inadequacies are entirely mine.

Gary Johns

April 2017

Brisbane

Previous works by Gary Johns

As Author

Aboriginal Self-determination: the Whiteman's dream (2010).

The Charity Ball: how to dance to the donors' tune (2014).

No Contraception, No Dole: tackling intergenerational welfare (2015).

Throw Open the Doors, The World Health Organization Framework Convention on Tobacco Control (2016).

As Editor

Right Social Justice: better ways to help the poor (2012).

Really Dangerous Ideas: what does and does not matter (2013).

Recognise What? (2014).

Contributed with a Chapter

Tim Wilson (ed), *Turning Left or Right: values in modern politics* (2013).

James Allan (ed), *Making Australia Right: where to from here?*

To purchase these books visit

www.connorcourt.com

or your local bookstore.

Contents

Table of Figures

1

Public health is new wine
in an old bottle

*The Australian government should follow the lead of France, Mexico,
the UK, and other countries in developing a policy for taxing and
subsiding foods and drinks to improve public health.*[1]

-- Linda Cobiac

The public health lobby in Australia, and around the world, says that
drinking, smoking, gambling, gluttonous fat slob 'sinners' are ruining
the nation. Stopping them would save billions of dollars. Neither of
these assertions is true. The public health lobby, a collection of health
and allied officials ensconced in health bureaucracies, universities
and non-government organisations (NGOs), acts as if your body
belongs to the nation. It does not. Listening to the lobby's advice,
some governments have moved well beyond protecting the taxpayer
from the costs imposed on others by those who, allegedly, make poor
choices in their personal consumption.

That governments restrict the choices of individuals for their

---

[1]   Linda Cobiac et al, 2017. Taxes and subsidies for improving diet and population
       health in Australia: a cost-effectiveness modelling study. *PLOS ONE* 14(2), 1.

own good is common.[2] It is also common that governments place additional obligations on those who live on welfare benefits. In both instances, a degree of regulation is justified where harm is obvious, its cause is direct and its effects irreversible, and the means of stopping the harm are not too taxing. But governments have begun to act as if your body belongs to them. They have become a parent, telling child-like citizens how to behave: instructing, forbidding, taxing and berating citizens about their personal choices. The degree of regulation is not justified in cases where the harm is not obvious or direct, or irreversible, and where the means of stopping the harm are too taxing.

There is a great deal of unjustified intervention – paternalism – in the name of public health. The result of paternalism is that sinners sometimes lose more than they gain; occasional indulgers and non-sinners almost always lose. Of course, taxpayers are vitally interested in the expense imposed by sinners on others – spillover costs are a real concern. Beyond that, trying to save people from themselves is a moral question. It should not involve the taxpayer. Trying to convince others to live better lives is the work of missionaries, not scientists. Public health experts should be disrobed of their scientific cloth and robed, instead, in sackcloth and ashes.

Public health is new wine in an old bottle. The old bottle is concern for the disadvantaged, for these are most likely to succumb to bad habits. The new wine is restricting and taxing everyone for indulging those habits. To paraphrase Australian economist Jonathan Pincus, the public health lobby are past masters at making "each person's decisions a matter of momentous financial consequence for others", which "gives them an excuse to control those decisions."[3]

---

[2]   Matthew Thomas and Luke Buckmaster, 2010. Paternalism in social policy: when is it justifiable? *Australian Parliamentary Library Research Paper no. 8 2010-11.*

[3]   As recalled by Henry Ergas, Sugar coating hard truths about obesity tax. *The Australian* 28 November 2016.

The public health activist's trick has been to argue that saving another is saving you money. This is not true. Public health activists make a number of errors in their advocacy. I have collected evidence to refute six of their major arguments for taxing and regulating sinful consumption, in effect, for owning your body. These can be summarised as follows:

1. Health care costs may not fall if unhealthy lifestyles are eliminated.

Comparing the lifetime health costs of obese people, smokers, and otherwise healthy-living people it was predicted that until the age of 56, yearly health costs are highest for obese people and lowest for healthy-living people. At older ages, the smoking group incurred the highest yearly costs.

However, because of differences in life expectancy (life expectancy at age 20 was five years less for the obese group, and eight years less for the smoking group, compared to the healthy-living group), total lifetime health spending was greatest for healthy-living people, lowest for smokers, and intermediate for obese people.[4]

2. Taxation is punitive when there is no health dividend.

Smoking prevalence rates in the last two decades have declined substantially from 25 per cent in 1991 to 13 per cent in 2013. Tobacco control measures implemented in Australia suggest the measures have had a substantial impact on the decline.

---

[4]   van Baal et al, 2008. Lifetime medical costs of obesity: prevention no cure for increasing health expenditure. *PLOS Medicine*, 0242.

They also suggest that a 'cultural revolution' based on better information, advertising bans (combat 'presence of mind' temptations) and inconvenience (banning indoor smoking) have been key. Tax increases appear to have come at the end of the culture change, after prevalence rates had dived.

3. Taxation is ineffective where the source of harm is diffuse.

An additional 20 per cent tax on sugar-sweetened beverages would save 1606 extra lives in the next 25 years.[5] Given that at least 3.7 million Australians will die in the next 25 years, 1606 seems a very small return on a considerable taxation measure.[6]

Australia has had a de facto sugar tax since 2000 with the introduction of the Goods and Services Tax, which taxes processed foods, leaving fresh foods untaxed. All the while, obesity has increased.

4. Estimating the cost of harm can be a fool's errand.

A 74 per cent rate of excise on alcohol could maximise net benefits to society, yielding $207 million per year in net benefits. This change of policy would result in an annual increase in excise and tax revenue to the Commonwealth government of $4.3 billion.

---

[5] Lennert Veerman et al, 2016. The impact of a tax on sugar-sweetened beverages on health and health care costs: a modelling study. *PLOS ONE* 11(4), 1. Two of the authors are employed by the Obesity Policy Coalition, which is funded by the Victorian Department of Health.

[6] Australian Institute of Health and Welfare, http://www.aihw.gov.au/deaths/ accessed 26 October 2016.

In careful language the researchers concluded, "the percentage increases in excise rates that are found to maximise net benefits to society are well above any changes that have been observed in practice."[7] It is a pretty peculiar world when a 74 per cent rate of tax is required to yield a net benefit. Back to the drawing board.

5. Arrogant strategies crowd out effective alternatives.

Public Health England found that "best estimates show e-cigarettes are 95 per cent less harmful to your health than normal cigarettes."[8] And yet the World Health Organization will not entertain an open discussion of harm reduction.[9]

It is understandable that public health advocates would not want to promote a harmful product, but to argue that "Even if e-cigarettes are significantly less harmful than conventional cigarettes, the product may have a very negative impact on public health if its use is spread to a large part of the population" says more about the values of the WHO than the science of public health.[10]

6. Public health competes with a host of other problems.

Public health officials find themselves in a world of pain when they face multiple complex problems, especially

---

[7] Marsden Jacob Associates, 2015. *Optimal Rates of Alcohol Taxation*, 20.
[8] Public Health England, 2015. *E-Cigarettes: An Evidence Update*, 5.
[9] C Bullen et al, 2013. Study protocol for a randomised controlled trial of electronic cigarettes versus nicotine patch for smoking cessation. *BMC Public Health* 13, 210.
[10] C Pisinger, 2014. Why public health people are more worried than excited over e-cigarettes. *BMC Medicine* 12, 226.

in developing countries. When lined up against other priorities for Bangladesh, newborn homecare and hypertension medicine were ranked well ahead of tobacco smoking and diabetes reduction.

None of these ranked anywhere near non-medical priorities. For example, Bangladeshi's are encouraged to stop burning cigarettes and dung, but not coal. And yet coal may be the one thing they need to burn to a point where they can stop burning cigarettes and dung. They may, in time, also need to burn calories, but first things first.

Several decades ago I read the book, *Four Arguments for the Elimination of Television.*[11] It failed to mention one good reason for television. Consumers want it. It might be an idea to keep an eye on the public health lobby. No politician should be giving away taxpayers' dollars for their schemes without solid proof of what they get in return.

---

[11] Jerry Mander, 1978. *Four Arguments for the Elimination of Television.* New York: HarperCollins.

2

Weighty problems of the public health lobby

Preventive health is not about a nanny state, it's not about taking away people's choices ... (but) Australians make bad choices about the food they eat, the fluids they drink and their level of physical activity every day. There are simply not enough public health campaigns.[12]

-- Dr Michael Gannon, Australian Medical Association

Okay, Dr Gannon, so people make bad choices. I agree, and some interventions such as banning tobacco advertising and sponsorship and taxation to discourage a habit that can kill seem reasonable. Maybe new measures to stem drunkenness in nightspots to prevent violence, or removing ATMs from poker machine outlets to curb problem gamblers, also seem reasonable, but controlling the eating habits of adults and children? There is a challenge. Banning, taxing, forbidding, and much else of the armoury of government regulation are very strong interventions. But applying these to food is bound to cause a reaction, and have unintended consequences. Worse, the evidence of how much of the wrong food causes harm is not clear.

---

[12] Michael Gannon, Health: the best investment that a nation can make. 17 August 2016 *National Press Club Address*, Canberra.

Two things have happened in developed countries in the last thirty years. Obesity and morbid obesity rates have increased because the typical adult consumes more calories, more protein, more fat, and more sodium than the typical adult in the 1970s.[13] The explanation is that calorie intake rises with income. It may also be accompanied by a change in the mix of foods, for example, a rise in the shares of fats, and sugar, but also fruit and vegetables.[14] In addition, in some countries, such as the US, the size of groups who are overweight, such as the poor, grew, and the size of groups less likely to be overweight, contracted. In other countries, for example, Australia, the number of poor has declined, but nevertheless obesity, especially childhood obesity, has increased among the poor. Everyone eats more, but the poor (who are not so poor anymore) eat even more, and more of the wrong foods.

As a recent McKinsey study concluded, 'obesity is a complex, systemic issue with no single or simple solution.'[15] But that does stop people trying. Take a look at the regulatory menu, "'Smart' food policies for obesity prevention" (featured in the box, 'Smart' food policies). The menu is a complete takeover of a child's life – from 'protecting' breastfeeding, to 'restricting' unhealthy food in school tuckshops, to 'forcing' healthy food into low-income neighbourhoods.

---

[13] United States figures. Ashley Kranjac and Robert Wagmiller, 2016. Decomposing trends in adult body mass index, obesity, and morbid obesity, 1971-2012. *Social Science and Medicine* 167, 43.

[14] Mario Mazzocchi and W. Bruce Traill, 2011. Calories, obesity and health in OECD countries. *Applied Economics* 43(26), 3926.

[15] McKinsey Global Institute, 2014. Overcoming obesity: an initial economic analysis. *Discussion Paper*, 1.

'Smart' food policies for obesity prevention

Provide an enabling environment for healthy preference learning
- Protection and promotion of breastfeeding
- Regulation of the marketing of inappropriate complementary foods to parents
- National provision of nutrition counselling to pregnant women and new parents
- Nutrition education for children, teachers and catering staff
- Initiatives to make healthy foods available in schools
- Food standards in schools that make healthy food available and restrict unhealthy foods
- Reformulation to reduce the sugar content in foods targeted at the child market
- Subsidise nutritious foods among low-income parents with young children
- Regulation of unhealthy food marketing to children
- Regulation of claims made on unhealthy foods that mislead children and their parents
- 'Zoning out' unhealthy food retail in places where children gather.

Overcome barriers to expression of healthy preferences
- Initiatives to make specific healthy foods available in schools
- Community and homestead gardening projects
- Community-based interventions that emphasise social participation and social networks
- Home delivery of healthy foods and meals to the elderly
- Targeted food subsidies
- Incentives to attract retailers of healthy foods into underserved low-income neighbourhoods
- Nutrition labels that fill information gaps.

Encourage people to reassess existing unhealthy preferences at point-of-purchase
- Health-related food taxes
- Targeted food subsidies implemented in the form of an incentive
- Standards that restrict foods from specific settings
- Redesigning of choice architecture at point-of-purchase
- Nutrition labels with some form of warning symbol or nutritional rating system.

Source: Corinna Hawkes et al, 2015. Smart food policies for obesity prevention. *The Lancet* 385(9985), 8.

Healthy eating is also coming to the workplace. The Victorian Department of Health has issued a healthy eating guide to workplaces. But it is more than a gentle nudge. It is a call to arms. It wants workers to "Seek management endorsement for implementing the Policy & Guide". The Department wants workers to: "Nominate a staff member, establish a new committee or use an existing committee to help plan and manage implementation of the Policy & Guide."[16] A call to arms, indeed, as long as the boss pays. And since when has it been policy to tell bosses to tell workers how to eat?

Perhaps an alarm should be sounded every morning to raise citizens from their slumber and harangue them into a stiff round of calisthenics? Perhapsf governments should assign a nutritionist, and a social worker, to every citizen? Mind you, and wouldn't you just know, some research suggests that the intensive activity meant to get you fit, may make you unhappy. "It is not obvious that encouraging all individuals to undertake higher intensity activity for longer will have the desired policy effect proposed by champions of the need to increasing the intensity of physical activity in the population."[17] Having fun with friends in 'active leisure' may do more good.

Is obesity a public health issue?

The five highest rating television episodes in Britain in 2016 were five episodes of The Great British Bake Off. There were 13 million viewers throughout Britain for each episode. You think that Brits are not obsessed with food? In Australia, Zumbo's Just Desserts, MasterChef and Nigella Bites are popular television shows. Australians, too, love food. There is, however, a down side. Too

---

[16] Department of Health Victoria, Prevention and Population Health Branch, 2013. *Healthy Choices: Healthy Eating Policy and Catering Guide for Workplaces*, 5.

[17] Paul Downward and Peter Dawson, 2016. Is it pleasure or health from leisure that we benefit from most? An analysis of well-being alternatives and implications for policy. *Social Indicators Research* 126(1), 460.

many Brits, Aussies and many more are fat slobs.

If we are what we eat, what are we if we are obese? Are the obese architects of their own demise? If so, why should anyone come to his or her aid? Indeed, the reason why anyone invests in harm prevention is to save themselves, not others. Diseases that stem from self-harm are not your problem, unless you are forced to pay for them. And yet, huge preventive measures are prescribed to prevent the obesity 'epidemic' as if it were your problem. A British government minister, for example, has berated the entire UK food industry for serving 'large portions' at restaurants and fast-food outlets.[18] Has it come to this? Blame industry for gluttony?

Obesity is a public health problem in one respect only: if the harm of obesity affects others. The only way it does is because of pooled insurance, which is why public health advocates want obesity categorised as a disease.[19] For example, to be a Health Promotion Charity in Australia it is not sufficient for a charity "to promote appropriate weight reduction or increased physical activity, without identifying the disease(s) that are being prevented or controlled through this promotion activity."[20] Awarding obesity disease status would allow obesity advocates to get on with their remedies without proving links to disease. Obesity would become everyone's problem and allow such charities, and other interested parties, free rein to expand their remit. Such a stance would also be in the interests of those organisations that have an interest in anti-obesity measures. In 2014, the principal financial supporters for the annual conference of the public health advocacy NGO, Obesity Australia, were, among others, iNova pharmaceuticals, BUPA Foundation, Weight

---

18   Chris Smyth, Restaurants ordered to reduce size of puddings. *The Times* 30 September 2016.

19   The NGO Obesity Australia's 2016 summit was titled, Is Obesity a Disease? Obesity Australia is a health promotion charity.

20   Australian Charities and Not-for-profits Commission, 2015. Commissioner's interpretation statement: health promotion charities. *CIS 2015/01*, 4.

Watchers, Novo Nordisk, and Allergen Australia. Obesity Australia lists one of its activities as 'political advocacy'.

It also follows that Medicare would cover the condition (conditions caused by obesity would, of course, in any event, be covered) and taxpayers would pay for it. All semblance of personal responsibility would disappear. By the way, guidelines for reporting obesity suggest that writers use the term 'people with obesity', rather than 'obese people', to guard against prejudicial statements such as 'the people who are overweight or obese have no self-control.'[21] Spot the difference: 'it is not my fault, my "obesogenic environment" made me do it!' It is not beyond possibility that, in the near future, mandatory reporting of severe childhood obesity will lead to children being taken from parents.[22] But that bespeaks incompetent parents, not a universal call to arms to stop an obesity epidemic.

What if it turns out that obese people, apart from those with some actual underlying medical cause, are simply those who show lack of restraint in an era when food is cheaper and more readily available than it has ever been? This would explain the recent and sudden surge in obesity much better than some disease-related explanation. And if certain people are more vulnerable than others, to what extent should others intervene to help, and at what cost?

This is where the fun and games begin. The annual cost of obesity in Australia has been estimated variously at between $37 billion and $58 billion a year.[23] But much of the so-called cost of obesity is loss of well-being. These losses are not a cost to society but to individuals. That part, which is shared because of public

[21]   Obesity Australia, 2015. *Rethink Obesity: A Media Guide on How to Report on Obesity.* Sydney, 13.

[22]   Roger Magnusson, 2016. Is obesity a disease?: legal implications. *Obesity Australia Summit Papers.*

[23]   Stephen Colagiuri, 2016. Is obesity a disease?: economic implications. *Obesity Australia Summit Papers.*

health insurance, is of concern, but the awful truth about public 'harm prevention' or 'health promotion' programs with respect to many consumption problems is that there are no public savings.

The reason is that healthy, not unhealthy, lifestyles drive up health costs.[24] While some preventive activities, such as immunization of children and mandatory seat belts, can be cost saving, "hundreds of economic studies have shown that prevention in chronic diseases [such as those associated with obesity] usually adds to medical costs."[25] Improvement in health associated with the prevention of obesity is a worthwhile goal in itself, but it does not follow that the prevention of obesity reduces national spending on medical care.

Medical science and healthier living postpone the costs of disability and disease and pave the way for more expensive non-fatal conditions among very old people. People who do not smoke have lower annual healthcare costs but higher lifetime costs because of their longer life. They also incur much higher social security costs as a result of their extra pension years. The general taxpayer therefore saves money if other people smoke.[26] That short-term healthcare costs of unhealthy people are lower than the long-term healthcare costs of healthy people comes as quite a shock to the prevention industry.

Although public health advocates downplay the financial costs associated with healthy living and longer lives, it is important these costs be considered in the policy mix. If gains are few, the public has less return than expected on its investment in health promotion or harm prevention policies. Governments may tax, regulate, and bewail sinners, but doing so may not lower the taxpayers' burden.

---

[24] Christopher Snowdon, 2015. Death and taxes: why living longer costs money. Institute for Economic Affairs, *Discussion Paper* no. 67.

[25] Louise Russell, 2009. Preventing chronic disease: an important investment, but don't count on cost savings. *Health Affairs* 28(1), 42.

[26] Snowdon 2015, 23.

More important, the finding that the lifetime health costs of unhealthy lifestyles are less than healthy lifestyles means that the rationale for controlling the lives of those who choose to indulge has much less weight than previously argued. It seems that bad 'lifestyles' are not public property.

Getting better all the time

The contest for the public's health takes place at a time when Australians are living longer and healthier lives. A male born in 2010 can expect to live 80 years, while a female can expect to live 84 years. Born a century earlier, a male could expect to live to 55 years, a female to 59 years (figure 1). As important, the chance of living longer free of 'disability' continues to increase, so that the quality of a longer life is improved.[27] However, the length of time people are disability free varies between healthy lifestyle and unhealthy lifestyle, but more on that later.

Infant and child mortality were greatly reduced because diseases, especially deadly to infants and children, such as measles, smallpox, polio, TB and the like, were stopped by inoculation. Medical science was crucial so, too, was awareness and vigilance by mothers and carers. Adult mortality has been greatly reduced because ischaemic heart disease and cerebrovascular disease (and to a lesser extent cancers) have been reduced by improvements in treatment and in managing risk factors such as smoking.[28] Again, both medical science and consumer awareness of risk were crucial.

---

[27] Australian Bureau of Statistics, 2014. *Measures of Australia's Progress, 2013.*
[28] Australian Bureau of Statistics, 2007. *Australian Social Trends, 2006.*

Figure 1. Life expectancy at birth by sex, Australia

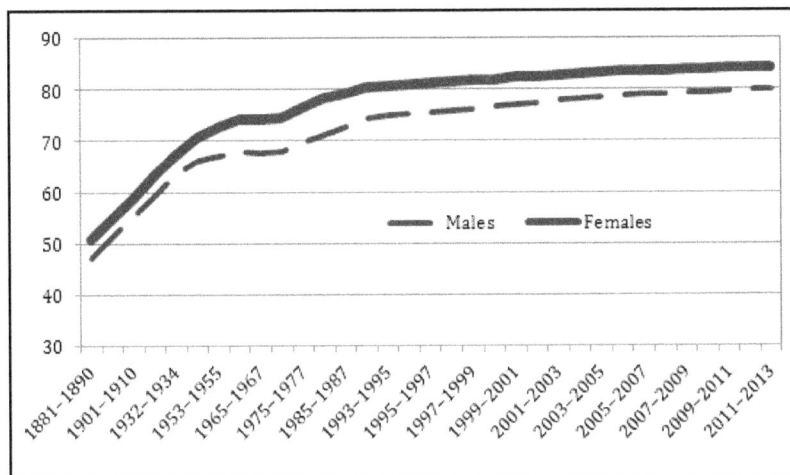

Source: ABS 2014. *Australian Historical Population Statistics, 2014.* ABS 2014. *Deaths, Australia, 2013*, table S.1.

There is also little doubt that interventions can reduce harm. Tobacco consumption has halved in the last 20 years (see figure 3) and alcohol consumption per capita, having risen substantially during the 1970s and 1980s, has returned to the levels of the 1960s.[29] The prevalence of problem gambling among the adult population has probably fallen since the 1990s.[30]

In other fields of behavioural concern it is possible to change for the better. Teenage pregnancy, for example, has fallen dramatically since 1975.[31] Accidents have also been a major source of early death and disability. The rate of death in Australia from fatalities at work

---

[29] Australian Bureau of Statistics, 2015. *Apparent Consumption of Alcohol, Australia* (series).
[30] Australian Productivity Commission, 2010. *Gambling.* Volume 1, Chapter 5.2.
[31] Australian Bureau of Statistics, 2015. *Births, Australia 2014*, Table 12.1.

or on the roads has fallen dramatically. In 2004, there were 3.5 deaths per 100,000 people in the employed civilian labour force. In 2014, the rate had fallen to 1.6 deaths per 100,000.[32] Key in these reductions were awareness and regulation. In 1970, there were eight road fatalities per 10,000 registered vehicles. In 2008, the rate had fallen to one.[33] Regulation, including legislation to reduce speed limits, the compulsory wearing of seat belts and testing driver competence, were crucial.

But how far can regulation go?

Your body belongs to the nation

National socialists, aka fascists, coined the slogan, "your body belongs to the nation".[34] The assumption is that each person has a duty to the nation to preserve his or her health.

I start from another point. Your body belongs to no one else but you. The only possible obligation to others for your health is to taxpayers for any cost they carry. The public health lobby, however, assumes that all costs associated with poor health are shared costs. This is not so, even in a relatively socialised public health system such as Australia's, where individuals meet around 17 per cent of all health care costs. The remainder is met by taxpayers through the public health system, by health fund members, and by employers through workers' compensation premiums.[35] So much of the debate around public health is to talk up the cost of health as if all of it were a cost to others.

---

[32] Australian Safety and Compensation Council, 2006. *Estimating the Number of Work-related Traumatic Injury Fatalities in Australia 2003-2004*, vii. Safe Work Australia, 2015. *Work-Related Traumatic Injury Fatalities, Australia 2014*, 5.

[33] Australian Bureau of Statistics, 2010. *Year Book Australia, 2009-10*.

[34] "Your body belongs to the nation" and "food is not a private matter" were exhortations in Nazi propaganda. Robert Proctor, 1999. *The Nazi War on Cancer*. New Jersey: Princeton University Press, 120.

[35] Australia's Future Tax System, 2009. *Final Report*. Part 2, chapter, e6-1.

Health insurance means pooling costs, and public health insurance, where premiums are not adjusted for past claims, means that a sick person will draw more heavily than a healthy person and not pay any more. Where illness is self-induced, there is an inescapable desire to have that person adjust their behaviour in the hope they draw less from the pool. The logic is fine but, in practice often overstated. The cost of illness may be exaggerated, the cause of the illness may not be readily attributed to a single source, and the costs of that person against the taxpayer may be measured in non-health terms, for example, time spent drawing the pension. Another question is whether there is a cost effective way to stop the allegedly offending behaviour?

In the navy, becoming sunburnt was always regarded as a self-inflicted injury, and punishable. A sailor out of action with sunburn, or sunstroke, is not much use in a war. All mining companies in Australia have severe limits on consumption of alcohol and drugs by their workforces. Workers can be summarily dismissed for failing a drugs test. The policy is essential because of the risks associated with, and the huge costs of, the equipment used in mining.

Similarly strong obligations are placed on welfare recipients. In an attempt to stem spending on tobacco and alcohol, now trialled in Australia, some beneficiaries receive almost all of their benefit in the form of a cashless debit card.[36] But obligations for those not on welfare benefits, or in very specific employment, are an altogether different matter. For citizens, who are under no obligation to the state, the big question is to work out, whether, and how much of a burden, another's poor habits is, and how much good or harm is caused by public health prescriptions.

With smoking, drinking and, to a lesser extent, gambling, it is

---

[36] Department of Social Services. https://www.dss.gov.au/families-and-children/programmes-services/welfare-conditionality/cashless-debit-card-trial-overview accessed 22 October 2016.

possible to draw a direct line between habit and harm. You can see some payoff in some prevention. But food? As the anti-obesity menu suggests, that is asking a great deal. And what is it about smoking and drinking that irks? Is it harm, or is it that passive smoke and objectionable drinkers are annoying? In recent years, separating smokers and drinkers from others has played a major part in the regulatory offensive. But, can annoyance be argued for obesity? Is there such a thing as passive obesity? Does an obese person turn violent after a big night on the burgers?

Even in areas of obvious risk, some health regulations prove very costly, or difficult to enforce, and have little impact. For example, a study of child deaths by drowning in backyard pools in NSW (there are more than 340,000 backyard swimming pools in NSW) found that of the 54 deaths in the period 2007-2014, almost all of the pools had a fence, but did not have a functioning safety barrier, mostly problems with the gate or latch. Pool fences in NSW have been compulsory since 1992. In all cases of drowning, the carer was distracted by household chores or attending to other children, or responsibility for supervision was unclear.[37] Additional fencing requirements, brought into being some years after the initial provisions, showed a decline in average annual child drowning deaths in pools, from to 5.5 from 5.2, after a decade.[38] A cost-benefit analysis undertaken using these results concluded that "substantial additional resources" applied to swimming pool safety was not warranted.[39] It is rare for a consultant to call a halt to regulation.

I, too, am an advocate for some forms of intervention. For example, the evidence that children born into households living on

---

[37] Ombudsman New South Wales, Children Death Review Team, 2015. *Drowning Deaths of Children (Private Swimming Pools) 2007-2014.*

[38] New South Wales Office of Local Government, 2015. Swimming pool barrier requirements for backyard swimming pools in NSW. *Discussion Paper*, 6.

[39] NSW Office of Local Government 2015, 8.

welfare are more likely themselves to spend considerable periods on benefits is incontrovertible.[40] These children are more likely to exhibit all manner of health and behavioural problems far in excess of others (the class nature of poor health is taken up in chapter three).

The question is what to do about it. I have advocated that any woman receiving a benefit from government, for example, for unemployment, study allowance, or to care for children, should avoid falling pregnant. To fall pregnant in these circumstances would in effect break the contract to find work, study, or care for existing children. The only way to avoid becoming pregnant is for the woman to be administered a long acting reversible contraception. This form of intervention is temporary, inexpensive and harmless, and may have considerable payoff.[41] Nevertheless, many find it too invasive.

What to do about public health policy errors

Sensible debate in this area must always be based on the merit of the arguments. Nevertheless, such is the confidence of public health advocates that some have sought to claim special status as the voice of the public and resent any challenge to that status.[42] They also want taxpayer funds to boost their profile. In addition, such is the power of 'medical experts', that politicians are vulnerable to scare campaigns. As important, because hiding behind a health banner lowers the political cost of raising taxation, taxation prescriptions sometimes find a ready ear among politicians always on the prowl for more revenue.

---

[40] Deborah Cobb-Clark, 2010. Disadvantage across the generations. *Insights* 8, 45-49.

[41] Gary Johns, 2015. *No Contraception, No Dole: Tackling Intergenerational Welfare*. Brisbane: Connor Court.

[42] Clive Hamilton and Sarah Maddison, 2007. *Silencing Dissent: How the Australian Government is Controlling Public Opinion and Stifling Debate*. Sydney: Allen & Unwin. BBC News, Charities 'will be silenced' by new grant rules. 6 February 2016.

Advocates sometimes embellish their moral concerns with economics. They are entitled to their morals, but not their economics. They almost always discount the value of risky choices that people make. They misrepresent the situation in consumer choice, when losses are counted but not gains. They ignore the unintended consequences of tax and regulation, on both sinners and non-sinners. As a consequence of well-placed concerns and misplaced calculations they urge governments to set down rules to prevent, persuade or punish individuals from choosing what they want.

In the last two decades the forces of harm prevention have grown enormously: mostly off the back of successful campaigns to convince smokers of the known harm in cigarettes. Advocates now head down the tobacco road to regulate a string of other products and services, many of which are not so clear sources of harm nor so amenable to change or better outcomes for all. Indeed, even with tobacco regulation, there is overreach in regulation and taxation. Anti-harm lobbies have gathered their forces, mainly under the banner of public health officials and activists, to tackle other sources of harm, which consumers knowingly choose. It is high time to look at the advocates and their arguments to see whether they warrant a little scrutiny of their own.

3

Why the public health lobby
make errors

I for my part am convinced that the day will come when international health law will contain rules at eliminating drunkenness, alcoholism and tobacco use ...[43]

-- Prof V S Mihajlov (former Union of Soviet Socialist Republics)

Okay, Professor Mihajlov, eliminating things seems to be a Russian past-time. In liberal democracies, it is a touch more difficult. Elimination is rarely an option. Public health advocates are more likely to aim for harm reduction. The more enthusiastic can stray into prescriptions for elimination. Medically trained people, and allied interested parties, see a role for their skills to help solve problems of personal consumption that have medical consequences. As a result, public health has a degree of untouchability. If a doctor diagnoses a problem and prescribes a remedy, the prescription carries weight. But, *public health* is not private health. Many individuals who knowingly choose to undertake harmful consumption are not diseased. They are free to make assessments of pleasure and pain, reward and risk.

---

[43]   A 1989 statement, quoted in World Health Organization Framework Convention on Tobacco Control, 2009. *History of the WHO Framework Convention on Tobacco Control*, 2.

Public health advocates are keen to make every health issue, everyone's issue. 'Scorned' lifestyles are now identified as noncontagious epidemics. An epidemic most commonly refers to the widespread occurrence of infectious disease, but it also can be defined as a "widespread occurrence of an undesirable phenomenon." The latter, however, is very different to public health, defined as the science of "understanding, mapping and containing contagious disease."[44] If there is no contagious disease, merely the undesirable phenomena of individuals choosing 'harmful' products such as tobacco, alcohol and some foods, it does not follow that science can prescribe a remedy. There is no inoculation for bad choices.

Tobacco road

Public health can make errors when it chases the success of earlier public health campaigns such as tobacco regulation. Tobacco regulation includes removal of corporate property rights over advertising and labelling, compulsory supply of health information to consumers, and heavy taxation of consumers. It also provides protection for non-smokers from annoyance and possible harm. These measures are used as a template for the regulation of other consumer items, almost all of which are less harmful.

The brilliant advertisement from the Diabetes Association of Sri Lanka (figure 2), which displays raw sugar and white sugar in the shape of a filtered cigarette, compares death rates for tobacco and sugar. There are doubts about the equivalence – a recent study found that "focusing public health messages on sugar may mislead on the need to reduce fat and overall energy consumption" but nevertheless the intention is clear.[45] Making sugar out to be as harmful as tobacco is powerful marketing.

---

[44] Pierre Lemieux, 2015. The dangers of 'public health'. *Regulation* Fall, 32.
[45] J J Anderson, 2016. Adiposity among 132 479 UK Biobank participants; contribution of sugar intake vs other macronutrients. *International Journal of Epidemiology* July 2016, 2.

Figure 2. When you're on a good thing, stick to it

The words read ...

> Tobacco is highly addictive. You love the way it makes you feel, the satisfaction it gives. You crave it. You need it to get through the day. It stimulates an integral part of your brain. It silently narrows your blood vessels, leading to more complications like heart disease and stroke. Somewhere in the world, it takes a life every six seconds.
>
> Sugar is highly addictive ... Somewhere in the world, it takes a life every six seconds.

Source: Diabetes Association of Sri Lanka, (http://adsoftheworld.com).

And others want to get in on the act too. Proceedings of a workshop in 2012 on 'climate accountability' posed the question, "What is the cancer of climate change." The workshop sought to compare the evolution of public attitudes and legal strategies related to tobacco control with those related to anthropogenic climate change. The tobacco road for NGOs is, "what is the cancer of [your product] we have to focus on?"[46] The cancer in this instance is obesity. Scientists are making explicit links between over indulgence and climate change, and recommending, for instance, that cutting excess consumption will save greenhouse gas emissions.[47]

---

[46] S Shulman, 2012. Establishing accountability for climate change damages: lessons from tobacco control. *Union of Concerned Scientists*, 6.

[47] Gillie Hendrie et al, 2014. Greenhouse gas emissions and the Australian diet: comparing dietary recommendations with average intakes. *Nutrients* 6, 289.

A prescription to tax motor vehicles and fuel more is especially heroic. The grounds are that cars and petrol are 'obesogenic and polluting'. 'Fats and sugars' are to be taxed because they are 'obesogenic'; more tax would bring back manual jobs to increase physical activity. [48]

These solutions suggest reversion to a pre-industrial economy, which, all other things being equal, would result in greater poverty and shorter lives. These attempts to rope in all manner of harm, medical and political, are symptomatic of a movement that has forsaken its expertise and has entered the world of ideology and politics.

Saving people from their own actions, however, has become a huge preoccupation of government and non-government organisations. Each delights in setting targets. In Australia, the National Preventative Health Taskforce, established in 2008 to develop a strategy on obesity, tobacco and alcohol, set a number of prevention targets. The strategy outlined 32 alcohol-specific actions and 27 obesity-specific actions. Governments love to do these things. The trouble is, a 2013 review by the Foundation for Alcohol Research and Education (FARE) found that only four actions had been completed and 18 were progressing on alcohol, and no progress had been made against ten, mostly obesity related, actions.[49]

Governments often chase their tail in these endeavours. For example, FARE is a 'health promotion' charity that declared an income of $3.3 million in 2015.[50] It was established in 2001 with a $115 million grant from the Australian Government to distribute

---

[48] Melanie Lowe, 2014. Obesity and climate change mitigation in Australia: overview and analysis of policies with co-benefits. *Australian and New Zealand Journal of Public Health* 38(1), 20.

[49] Rob Moodie et al, 2016. Australia's health: being accountable for prevention. *Medical Journal of Australia* 204(6), 223.

[50] Foundation for Alcohol Research and Education, 2015. *Annual Financial Report 2014-15*, 10.

funding for programs and research that aimed to prevent the harms caused by alcohol and licit substance misuse. In 2011, the Chief Executive Officer stated that FARE had "moved from a grant making body, to becoming a proactive and strategic ... advocate and organiser of the efforts to reduce alcohol misuse in Australia."[51] I have elsewhere labelled this circular event 'the charity ball', whereby government funds advocates, with charity status, to lobby government for preferred policy solutions.[52]

But even tobacco regulation has its blind spots. In their zeal to eliminate a legal product some regulators close the door to less harmful products for those who persist in the habit. Governments sometimes use the opportunity to gouge consumers (tax the consumer more than is necessary to recover the cost of harm to others), and escape opprobrium, because they are seen to be saving people from harm.

Sometimes those in the public health business focus on harm, and ignore a rational assessment of rewards associated with choice. Sometimes, they prefer the elimination of a particular source of harm, despite the fact that a consumer may want to pursue that activity knowing the risks. Even when the consumer has difficult choices, because of addiction, the harm prevention advocate nevertheless pursues goals intended to wipe out the activity, with little hope of achieving it. A more sensible approach, in almost all cases, is to have the consumer face the risks and the rewards of consumption. Or, where an intervention seems warranted, evaluate the effectiveness of any measure to ensure that the cost never outweighs the benefit in the curtailment of risky behaviour.

---

51 Foundation for Alcohol Research and Education, 2012. *Annual Report 2011-12*, 1.
52 Gary Johns, 2014. *The Charity Ball: How to Dance to the Donors' Tune.* Melbourne: Connor Court.

Change society!

The Tasmanian Government has a goal to make Tasmania the healthiest population in Australia by 2025. Tasmanians are among the least healthy Australians, after Northern Territorians, with high rates of chronic disease and health risk factors like smoking, obesity, poor nutrition, low levels of physical activity, and risky alcohol consumption.[53] The strategy, and urging for the 'goal', came from the public health lobby, Health and Wellbeing Advisory Council, and from the Health Council of Tasmania.[54] The strategy, still in development, among many things considered lifting the legal age for sale of cigarettes to 25 years, subsequently ruled out, and tripling the licence fee for tobacco retailers. The problem with such goals and strategies is that they are framed as if all people are the same. They are not.

The Australian Institute of Health and Welfare, for example, argue that, "if the poor were as healthy as the rich they would be 21 per cent better off."[55] They further argue that 30 per cent of the burden of disease (a measure that combines impact of dying early and living with illness) is caused by 'modifiable risk factors' and, therefore, is preventable.

An example of a modifiable risk factor is 'high body mass' — fat. It could lead to heart disease, diabetes and more. A great many modifiable risks are 'behavioural'. They are very familiar and include alcohol, tobacco, drugs, unsafe sex, physical inactivity, childhood sexual abuse, domestic violence, and a diet low in vegetables. All of these factors are heavily class based. The flaw in the association

---

[53] Tasmanian Government Department of Health and Human Services, http://www.dhhs.tas.gov.au/about_the_department/our_plans_and_strategies/a_healthy_tasmania accessed 29 December 2016.

[54] Will Hodgman Premier of Tasmania and Michael Ferguson, Minister for Health, A Healthy Tasmania. *Press release* 22 February 2015.

[55] Australian Institute of Health and Welfare, 2016. *Impact and Causes of Illness and Deaths in Australia 2011*, vii.

between health and income, however, is that there may be significant other reasons why the poor are poor and unhealthy.

It will not come as any surprise, for example, that all of these factors are intergenerational. Children, whose parents exercise, do not smoke or binge drink, are more likely to eat more fruit and vegetables and less energy-dense (junk) foods. By contrast, children of mothers with poor habits eat less fruit and vegetable. Unhealthy eating habits in children, which are likely to be maintained in adolescence and adulthood, are more likely to be male, from low income families, single-parent families, rural areas, have parents without a university degree, were not breastfed at six months of age, and have mothers with less healthy eating and lifestyle practices.[56]

The same study found that children in single-parent households watched more television, ate more food high in fat and sugar and less fresh fruit and vegetables than children from dual-parent households. The findings suggest that an additive effect of dietary and activity variables may contribute to the higher rates of overweight and obesity in Australian children, and that girls from single-parent households may be particularly at risk.[57]

The message in the reports is quite simple. If you change who you are, or the way you live, or with whom you live, you will live longer. The solutions, however, are not so simple. Such change would require massive intervention. Obesity Australia, for example, contends that "there is currently excellent animal experimental evidence for environmental effects on sperm and ova predisposing the offspring to obesity", and that "there is a wealth of evidence for a variety of causative factors during pregnancy (mother's obesity or

---

[56] Galina Daraganova and Lukar Thornton, 2013. Eating behaviour: socio-economic determinants and parental influence. *Longitudinal Study of Australian Children Annual Statistical Report 2013*, 91-110.

[57] Linda Byrne et al, 2011. Parental status and childhood obesity in Australia. *International Journal of Pediatric Obesity 6*, 415.

diabetes/not enough calories or protein/stress)."[58] The link between mother and child is, no doubt, crucial in identifying a proximate cause of childhood obesity. But what causes the mother's, or the parents', obesity? Is it relative income, absolute income, culture, welfare dependence, marital status, personality, or genes? And, if one or a combination of these factors could be isolated, what policies would solve the problem?

Obesity Australia also observe, again quite plausibly, that "over the first two to three years after birth a child's taste and food preferences are set, and can contribute to susceptibility in our current obesogenic environment."[59] Plausibly, Obesity Australia argues that a large number of people are susceptible to obesity, in an era when food is plentiful and cheap. For Obesity Australia, as for almost all preventive program advocates, the solution is to take children from poor environments and teach them those habits their parents do not. In some ways, this agenda is no different to that which created the public school system. That is, there are those who, left to their own devices, would be unable to afford to learn, or lack sufficient insight or intelligence, to acquire the skills and habits that would make them more able to succeed in general, and less susceptible to harm. The issue here is the resources that should be devoted in school curricula, and elsewhere, to such matters.

Such tasks would be likely to be fairly ineffectual or, at least, as ineffectual as any schools programs have been in eliminating differences in intelligence, personality, genes, and income, which is why other advocates seek more radical interventions. The Social Determinants of Health Alliance is a public health lobby group that uses the slogan, 'fair, just, right, equitable', and compiles a great deal of data that indicates a relationship between poor health and poverty. The *Alliance* asserts that inequality is a cause of poor health,

---

[58]   Obesity Australia 2013, *Action Agenda*, 4.
[59]   Obesity Australia 2013, 4.

and that, therefore, equality must be the solution.[60] Their intellectual leader is Michael Marmot who, in the introduction to a United Nations report, stated, "Health [inequity] ... is a matter of social justice and ... social injustice is killing people on a grand scale."[61] Marmot expounded his theories at great length in Australia in the 2016 Boyer Lectures.[62] Unfortunately, Marmot and his Australian followers have no idea how to fix the problem other than tackle the "inequitable distribution of power, money, and resources", which either means to lobby for further transfers of income from one group to another or for some kind of socialist revolution. Both have their shortcomings.

Perhaps the most emblematic of heroic public health advocacy is the Health in All Policies Collaboration, a name that suggests that medical and allied professionals see all problems through medical lenses.[63] Their skills are used to reinforce a pre-existing ideology, that is, that a more equal society is a more healthy society. Even if this were true, it would take a long time to achieve and many patients could die waiting.

The Australian Institute of Health and Welfare has a more sober view. It acknowledges the concept of social determinants of health and that it can be used as a platform for interventions in some policy fields – transport, housing, environmental, educational, social and so on, but cautions that health determinants also vary in how modifiable they are.[64] The more 'upstream' (social) determinants, such as education, employment, income and family structure, can be

---

60 Social Determinants of Health Alliance, http://socialdeterminants.org.au accessed 23 October 2016.
61 Commission on Social Determinants of Health, 2008. *Closing the Gap in a Generation*, i.
62 Australian Broadcasting Commission, Fair Australia: social justice and the health gap. *2016 Boyer Lectures.*
63 Maxim Gakh, 2015. Law, the health in all policies approach, and cross-sector collaboration. *Public Health Reports* 130(1), 96-100.
64 Australian Institute of Health and Welfare, 2012. *Australia's Health 2012*, 13.

too difficult and complex to modify successfully.

Modification for the more 'downstream' determinants can be more specific, for example, programs and policies aimed at influencing health behaviours – legislation against tobacco smoking in cars with children, restricting alcohol sales to young people, and enforcing the wearing of seat belts – help to reduce the burden of illness and injury. The distinction between action and inaction has to be made on the basis of the effectiveness and cost, including to the consumer, of the particular restriction. Where effectiveness is unproven or minor and cost is significant, public health is no more than an exercise in changing society: not for the faint hearted, and not particularly suited to the medical profession.

Why blame inequality?

The AIHW could also have said, but this would be too controversial for a government agency, that personality traits, such as conscientiousness and agreeableness, affect employment prospects, which, in turn, determine income and health. They affect, for example, how keen individuals are to turn up to work on time, to do what they are told, to be polite to customers, and to cooperate with colleagues.[65] Unfortunately, "welfare claimants on average possess a personality profile that is less conscientious and agreeable than that of employed citizens."[66] Welfare claimants are less likely to be employed, and the unemployed have poorer health.

Furthermore, poor language skills are a pathway for such a personality. Perkins notes that children from professional families hear an average of more than 2000 words per hour, compared to an average of more than 1000 words per hour for working class

---

[65] Adam Perkins, 2016. *The Welfare Trait: How State Benefits Affect Personality.* Palgrave Macmillan (electronic).

[66] Perkins 2016, 133.

children and an average of only 600 words per hour for the children of welfare claimants. The cumulative vocabulary of children is vastly different. The fact is, parents at the lower end barely speak to their children and, as a consequence, their schooling suffers. Just to give an idea of the immensity of the task of overcoming poor language skills, 60,000 children, or 20 per cent of children born in Australia, are born to a woman when she is on welfare benefits.[67] These children are more likely than others to have poor language skills.

Perkins believes that a "welfare state which increases the number of children born into disadvantaged households risks imposing a significant per capita headwind on society." Each of those children will, on average, "create a burden for the welfare state and the criminal justice system that is four times larger than the burden imposed by average individuals." More importantly, schooling has limited powers to change upbringing and none at all on genes. Even those children subject to a very expensive program of intensive preschool tutoring remain twice as likely as the rest of the population to fall back on welfare or be involved in crime. A crucial finding is the willingness among welfare recipients "to have extra children in order to increase welfare income, then to neglect those children."[68]

These insights may appear to be somewhat fatalistic, but the evidence is solid. There is little point in wishing and hoping that everyone had the same propensity to make healthy choices or, indeed, to respond to information that would ensure they make sensible (to others) choices. Alas, it is not so. But there are alternative, or perhaps additional, reasons for poor choices and habits. Others attribute an extraordinary range of societal problems among the rich and poor to scarcity – not to the attributes of the person, but to the context of the scarcity under which they operate. Scarcity raises the cost of

---

[67] Johns 2015, 130.
[68] Perkins 2016, 2473.

error because it operates like a tax; it provides more opportunity to make misguided choices because many operate with a very narrow or tunnel vision.

Choices based on a focus on the immediate future and made under taxing conditions can be disastrous. Diabetics, for example, take their medication only 50 to 70 per cent of the time. Brilliant pharmacology comes to nought because someone forgot to take their tablet. More broadly, the "poor in the United States who are on Medicaid pay nothing for their medications, yet they fail to take them regularly." The poor are worse parents. They are harsher with their children, less consistent, more disconnected and thus "are more likely to take out their own anger on the child." Further, "poor women are less likely to eat properly or engage in prenatal care (regardless of availability of food and medicine)."[69]

The startling conclusion is that just as failure causes poverty, poverty causes failure. Many public health programs rely on the poor to absorb new information. Campaigns try to educate the public about the importance of eating healthier, smoking less, obtaining prenatal care, and so on. So much of these changes require individual discipline and self-control, which the poor may not have. This is not a moral observation, rather it is an observation of people who are, literally, taxed by their circumstances such that they lack the foresight to make sound judgements in their best interest. The big message from this research is that programs, rewards and penalties to help the poor must be focussed on immediate needs and behaviours, not the long-term needs that require planning and foresight. Socialists may prick up their ears at these insights but, alas, their solution is useless, there will never be enough resources. The poor in the first world are wealthy compared to the third world, and ever so much better off than the wealthy of earlier generations.

---

[69]   Sendhil Mullainathan and Eldar Shafir. 2015. *Scarcity: The True Cost of Having Nothing.* Penguin (electronic), 151.

But how much can government intervene in the lives of others? The barriers to change, in class and personality, are immense, and where is the payoff? For example, 'sin' taxes, to dissuade further purchases of harmful products, tax the poor more heavily, in relative terms, than the rich. The amounts of cash transferred between rich and poor in developed countries are immense. It is unlikely that equality will ever have sufficient payoff to solve the problems of health inequality. Public health has become a proxy for social engineering on a grand scale. A more dignified policy aim would be to ensure that the cost of harm to others is minimised or, as efficiently as possible, recouped. The sheer difficulty of changing people and societies should not become an excuse to meddle too much in too many lives.

How the public health lobby make errors

Public health advocates have a tendency to become social justice warriors. Their medical background, if they have one, and its attendant desire to save lives, fuses with the desire to save people from themselves, regardless of cost. But, at what point does the cost of a particular health, or harm prevention, strategy outweigh the benefits? Here are six clear examples where the cost of harm prevention is at risk of outweighing the benefits.

Each is analysed in chapters to follow.

1. Health care costs may not fall if unhealthy lifestyles are eliminated.

    Compare lifestyle costs of health to lifetime costs of health.

2. Taxation is punitive when there is no health dividend.

    Taxation follows the fall in smoking rates.

3. Taxation is ineffective where the source of harm is diffuse.

    The sugar tax is not a cure for obesity.

4. Estimating the cost of harm can be a fool's errand.

    Harm estimates incorporate private loss, or ignore benefits.

5. Arrogant strategies crowd out effective alternatives.

    The UN Framework Convention on Tobacco Control is a closed shop.

6. Public health competes with a host of other problems.

    Choose your poison: to burn tobacco, dung, coal or calories.

4

Health care costs may not fall if unhealthy lifestyles are eliminated

Thirty years ago obesity may have been considered primarily a personal matter; today it is overwhelmingly a societal issue, given its prevalence and costs.[70]

-- Obesity Australia

Okay, Obesity Australia, it is fair to suggest that obesity is rampant and that there are associated health risks. Debate about the health risks associated with consumption, from tobacco and alcohol through sugar (and even fossil fuels), are squarely in the public arena. For example,

- 1 in 6 Australian adults smoke daily
- 1 in 5 Australian adults consume more than two standard drinks per day
- 1 in 2 Australian adults do not eat enough fruit
- 9 in 10 Australian adults do not eat enough vegetables
- 1 in 2 Australian adults are not sufficiently active.

As a result, and allowing that some Australians have biomedical predispositions, almost two in three Australian adults are overweight or obese.[71] Moreover, results from the 2011-12 Australian Health Survey show that 25 per cent of children aged 2-17 are overweight

---

[70] Obesity Australia 2013, 2.
[71] Australian Institute of Health and Welfare, *Risk Factors to Health*. http://www.aihw.gov.au/risk-factors/ accessed 14 September 2016.

or obese, with 18 per cent being overweight and seven per cent obese. The proportion of children and adolescents aged 5-17 who are overweight or obese increased between 1995 and 2007-08 (21 per cent and 25 per cent, respectively) but has remained stable to 2011-12 (26 per cent).[72] An overweight child is likely to become, and remain, an obese adult. I accept the data. I accept that obesity is harmful. But, its causes are multiple and not as amenable to 'fixes' as tobacco and alcohol.

More important, and this applies to all of the consumption sins, there may be no public savings in a 'cure'. Neither is obesity a 'societal' issue because, for it to be so, there has to be some problem that obese people create for non-obese people.

It is true that medical costs are shared through public medical insurance and that thereby obese people force these costs onto non-obese people, but to this problem there are two solutions. Obese people should carry more of their costs, thus relieving the burden on others. However, and most intriguing, by comparing lifestyle costs of health to lifetime costs of health, it is more likely that healthy, not unhealthy, lifestyles have driven up health costs.[73] So, the obese have less to be sorry for than is generally claimed.

The relationship between prevention and health-care spending is complex. Some preventive activities can be cost saving, especially those that are relatively cheap to implement and that prevent a condition that is generally non-fatal but expensive to treat. Examples include immunization of children and policies that prevent traffic accidents, such as mandatory seat belts. The prevention of fatal diseases, however, may actually lead to an increase in health-care spending. This is because the extra years of life generated inevitably result in an increased need for treatment of chronic conditions and

---

[72] Australian Institute of Health and Welfare, 2012. *Who is overweight?* http://www.aihw.gov.au/who-is-overweight/#children accessed 30 November 2016.

[73] Snowdon 2015, 7.

for long-term nursing care. Overall, most medical interventions designed to prevent disease or improve health cause an increase in health-care spending. This is not to argue against treatment, but to argue that cost savings touted by various advocates may not exist.

The awful truth is that there are no savings in it

Typical studies of the cost of obesity (and other sins) will generate large numbers. For example, the accounting firm Price Waterhouse Coopers estimated the total costs of obesity in Australia in 2011-12 to be $8.6 billion (2014-15 dollars). This total figure includes $3.8 billion in direct costs and $4.8 billion in indirect costs. Projections generate even bigger numbers, so that, for example, "there will be 2.4 million more obese people in 2025 than in 2011-12 and $87.7 billion in additional costs due to obesity to society over the ten years (2015-16 to 2024-25)."[74] The PwC study ignored any benefits.

A study by Buchmueller, which investigated the relationship between obesity and health care expenditure in Australia, observed that "to the extent that obesity leads to premature mortality, savings from a policy that successfully reduces obesity at younger ages may be partially offset by higher lifetime expenditures caused by increased longevity." This study, nevertheless, estimated that "interventions that are successful in reducing obesity rates may also have the effect of reducing health expenditures."[75] The PwC study counted costs but not the benefits of obesity; and the Buchmueller study counted the cost of health expenditure, but not formally other lifetime non-medical costs. Neither has the entire picture.

Whether interventions pay depends on measuring costs and benefits of the offending activity. With any study it is essential

---

[74]   Price Waterhouse Coopers. 2015. *Weighing the Cost of Obesity: A Case for Action*, iv and v.
[75]   Thomas Buchmueller and Johar Meliyanni, 2015. Obesity and health expenditures: evidence from Australia. *Economics and Human Biology* 17, 54.

to check whether all costs and benefits are factored. For example, Crampton's critique of a report by the Department of Health Victoria (featured in the box, Vic Health wrong estimates) on the costs of smoking points out multiple errors. The errors apply to all 'sin' products.

Vic Health wrong estimates of smoking benefits and costs

Eric Crampton critique of Vic Health

- Massively and inappropriately discounted the benefits of smoking, and included as a cost of smoking the resources that go into tobacco production. A gross measure of consumer surplus would be fine, but it was not included.[76]

- Counts the health care costs of a smoker dying at 63 of lung cancer against the health care costs of a non-smoker at 63. It takes no account that the smoker then does not, for example, impose other health care costs while dying of congestive heart failure at age 76. It essentially assumes that the smoker could have gone on living forever without health care costs absent the smoking.

- Acknowledges the fact that smoking correlates with other risk-taking behaviours, but ignores the fact that smoking costs may well be conflated with other risk-taking costs.

- Leaves aside that smokers, by dying early, cost the superannuation and pension system a whole lot less as well: they pay into the system but draw far less from the system.

- Ignores the fact that cigarette excise taxes are paid upfront while health care costs are far in the future. The young smoker, in effect, pays an annuity to the government to cover excess health costs 30 or 40 years in the future.[77]

Norman Temple provides an excellent illustration of how to take into account all costs associated with interventions designed to persuade people to quit smoking. He points out that many estimates of

---

[76] Eric Crampton, 2008. Cost-benefit analysis when the conclusion drives the method: a review of 'Report on Tobacco Taxation in New Zealand'. *The New Zealand Medical Journal* 121(1269), 91.

[77] Eric Crampton, Excess costs of smoking. *Offsetting Behaviour* 16 June 2010.

the cost to persuade people to stop smoking are seriously flawed.[78]

Consider a man, aged 40 years, who has smoked half a pack a day for the previous 20 years. Assume he continues smoking, and will die of coronary heart disease (CHD) at the age of 65 years. If he quits, however, he will live to 75 years and then die of CHD. Temple asks, what effect does quitting have on health-care spending? What are the other financial implications of a person ceasing to smoke? There are three ways to answer these questions.

The narrow view is to consider the next 25 years. The effect of quitting is clearly to reduce health-care spending. This is because prevention of death from CHD saves the cost of treating the man for terminal CHD. In addition, the man is likely healthier for those 25 years and therefore has less need for medical treatment.

The longer-term view is to consider the next 35 years. The man dies at the age of 75 years from terminal CHD, so the cost of treatment has not been avoided but merely postponed. Moreover, the savings brought about by improved health before the age of 65 years are likely to be cancelled out, perhaps even exceeded, by the increased health-care spending that typically occurs with people aged over 65 years. The savings in health-care spending are illusionary.

The 'big picture' perspective considers non-medical expenditures. Because the man in the above example did not smoke between the age of 40 and 65 years, he paid nothing in tobacco taxes during those years. Taxpayers therefore lose considerable revenue. In addition, he almost certainly receives an age pension. The taxpayers, through the government, must therefore pay additional monies for the 10 extra years he lives after the age of 65 years.

From a taxpayer perspective, the effect of this man quitting smoking at the age of 40 years is two-fold. Each dollar in savings

[78] Norman Temple, 2012. Why prevention can increase health-care spending. *European Journal of Public Health* 22(5), 618.

that occurs before the age of 65 years leads to a dollar or more of spending after the age of 65 years. There is a significant negative impact on government finances from the double effect of lost tax revenues combined with increased spending on pension payments.

Temple cautions that under different scenarios at older ages, prevention may allow a longer life, less disability, without increased health-care costs and that prevention can also be much more cost-effective than medical treatments. But, over the past 40 years, hundreds of economic studies have shown that prevention in chronic diseases such as heart disease and stroke, and diabetes, as well as for screening for various cancers, and in the management of chronic conditions, usually adds to medical spending.[79]

Obesity prevention, for example, may not result in cost savings. Although effective obesity prevention leads to a decrease in costs of obesity-related diseases, this decrease is offset by cost increases because of diseases unrelated to obesity in life-years gained. The study by van Baal, in the Netherlands, compared the lifetime health costs of obese people, smokers, and otherwise healthy-living people. The study predicted that until the age of 56, yearly health costs are highest for obese people and lowest for healthy-living people. At older ages, the smoking group incurred the highest yearly costs. However, because of differences in life expectancy (life expectancy at age 20 was five years less for the obese group, and eight years less for the smoking group, compared to the healthy-living group), total lifetime health spending was greatest for healthy-living people, lowest for smokers, and intermediate for obese people.[80]

Although public health advocates downplay the financial costs associated with healthy living and longer lives, it is important these costs be considered in the policy mix. If gains are few, the public has

---

[79]   Russell 2009, 42.
[80]   van Baal et al 2008, 0242.

less return than expected on its investment in health promotion or harm prevention policies.

Morbidity: Compression or expansion?

An important consideration in these calculations of lifetime health costs is the cost of care at the very late stages of life. The 'compression of morbidity' occurs if the age at first appearance of aging manifestations and chronic disease symptoms can increase more rapidly than life expectancy. The question of whether the period of morbidity may be shortened depends on whether the average onset age of a marker of morbidity (first heart attack, first dyspnea from emphysema, first disability from osteoarthritis, first memory loss) can increase more rapidly than does life expectancy from the same age. If it does, then the period between that marker and the end of life is shortened.

Absolute compression of morbidity occurs if age-specific morbidity rates decrease more rapidly than age-specific mortality rates. Relative compression of morbidity occurs if the amount of life after first chronic morbidity decreases as a percentage of life expectancy.[81] Three broad health scenarios have been proposed to describe the evolution of mortality, morbidity and disability and the health consequences of increasing life expectancy at older ages (featured in the box, Three scenarios of morbidity).

An analysis by the Australian Institute of Health and Welfare did not find any evidence of absolute expansion of disability for older Australians from 1998 to 2012. The gains in life expectancy at age 65 years were accompanied by increases in the expected years both with and without disability or severe or profound core activity limitation.

---

[81] James Fries, 2005. The compression of morbidity. *The Milbank Quarterly* 83(4), 810.

From 1998 to 2012, in Australia, life expectancy at birth increased for both sexes, and most of this increase corresponded with an increase in years free of disability and severe or profound core activity limitation (that is, sometimes or always needing personal help with activities of self-care, mobility or communication). The disability-free life expectancy for males increased by 4.4 years, which was more than the gain in male life expectancy (4 years). For females, years free of disability increased by 2.4 years.

Australian boys born in 2012 could expect to live an average of 62.4 years without disability and another 17.5 years with some form of disability, including 5.6 years with severe or profound limitation of core activity. Girls born in 2012 could expect to live 64.5 years without disability and another 19.8 years with some form of disability, including 7.8 years with severe or profound limitation of core activity.

Males at age 65 in 2012 could expect to live an average 8.7 years without disability and another 10.4 years with some form of disability, including 3.7 years with severe or profound limitation of core activity. Females at age 65 could expect to live 9.5 years without disability and another 12.5 years with some form of disability, including 5.8 years with severe or profound limitation of core activity.

Three scenarios of morbidity

Compression of morbidity

- The period living with ill-health and disability before death is shortened because of a delay in onset of chronic disease or disability and a slowdown in the rate of increase in life expectancy

- If the number of expected years of life with disability falls, there is an absolute compression of morbidity

- If the proportion of expected years of life with disability falls without the number of expected years of disability decreasing (it could even rise), there is a relative compression of morbidity.

Expansion of morbidity

- Increasing longevity is accompanied by more survivors who are frail and suffer from chronic conditions, resulting in a longer period living with disability before death

- If the number of expected years of life free of disability falls, there is an absolute expansion of morbidity

- If the proportion of expected years free of disability falls without the number of expected disability-free years decreasing (it could even rise) there is a relative expansion of morbidity.

Dynamic equilibrium

- The overall level of diseases or disability increases largely due to the increase of less severe diseases or disability, while the prevalence of severe diseases or disability falls or remains stable, due to the rate of progression of disease or disability slowing down

- If the ratio of disability-free life expectancy to total life expectancy is constant, there is equilibrium

- For the severity of disability, if the number of years with disabilities – all levels combined – increases, while the number of years with severe disability remains constant or even falls within life expectancy, there is said to be 'dynamic equilibrium'.

Source: The Australian Institute for Health and Welfare, 2014. Healthy life expectancy in Australia: patterns and trends 1998 to 2012. *Bulletin 126*, 19.

The gains in the number of expected years living free of disability were related to a combination of increasing longevity and decreases in prevalence rates of disability. There is also no consistent evidence suggesting the 'dynamic equilibrium' scenario for older Australians, because the expected years with severe or profound core activity limitation continued to increase slightly in 1998-2012, along with the increase in the years with disability as a whole. During 1998-2012, there is also no evidence of absolute compression of disability among older Australians, irrespective of the level of disability. At age 65, gains in the expected years free of disability and severe or profound core activity limitation were not greater than the gains in life expectancy. Gains in longevity were accompanied by increases in the expected years of disability as well as severe or profound limitation of core activity.

These findings confirm that no single scenario applies in Australia over the study period; instead, a combination of positive and negative changes is evident, consistent with recent international experience.[82] This suggests that there is no impending solution to the cost of ageing in, for example, lower smoking and drinking rates experienced in Australia over a number of decades. Obesity prevention, given its many causes, may be even less promising.

As for the non-health costs of ageing, James Fries, a leader in ageing research advocates that "there should be no mandatory retirement age" in order to maintain health in old age.[83] But, the fact is that there is, or at least an age at which retirement benefits become available, and it is inconceivable that a pension will not be available at an age relatively young compared to the rising rate of longevity. In 2012, life expectancy at age 65 (that is, the number of additional years a person at age 65 could expect to live) was 19.1 years (to 84.1) for males and 22.0 years (to 87.0) for females. The pension eligibility age as of 2012 was 65 for men and 64.5 for women.

In 1960, for example the life expectancy for men at age 65 was 77.5 and for women at age 65 was 80.7. The pension age was 65 and 60 respectively. In 1960, a man could expect to be on the aged pension for 11.5 years and a woman 20.7 years. In 2012, a man could expect be on the age pension for 19 years and a woman 22.5 years.[84] The non-health lifetime costs of ageing are increasing.

---

[82] The Australian Institute for Health and Welfare, 2014. Healthy life expectancy in Australia: patterns and trends 1998 to 2012. *Bulletin 126*, 19.

[83] Fries 2005, 819.

[84] The Australian Institute for Health and Welfare 2014, 1.

Underestimating the financial costs of healthy longer lives

It is good to be wary of any study that purports to show that there is a saving in harm prevention or health promotion. These may be beneficial, but they often come with a price tag. Snowdon provides a handy checklist of the ways public health advocates downplay the financial costs of healthy longer lives.

- Focusing on end-of-life health costs while ignoring the additional-years-of life health costs

- Paying little attention to long-term care costs, which are greater than the acute healthcare costs associated with ageing

- Ignoring welfare payments

- Focusing on per capita costs rather than the ratio of working taxpayers to pensioners

- Arguing that facilitating healthy ageing will reduce healthcare costs.[85]

The rationale for gouging taxation, as is the case with tobacco excise, or restricting access, as is the case with alcohol, or highly interventionist programs as is the case with food labelling, is a lot shakier when public health interventions are not a saving. Governments may tax, regulate, and bewail sinners, but doing so will not lower the taxpayers' burden. The rationale for controlling the lives of those who choose to indulge has a lot less weight than previously argued. It seems that 'lifestyles' are not public property.

---

[85]   Snowdon 2015, 30.

5

Taxation is punitive when there is no health dividend

We will implement a further four annual 12.5 per cent increases in tobacco excise, with the first increase to take effect on 1 September 2017. The net impact of the tobacco measures will raise $4.7 billion over the next four years.[86]

-- Hon. Scott Morrison, Treasurer of Australia

Okay, Scott Morison, how many smokers will quit as a result of your taxes, announced in the 2016 Budget? As members of the government backbench cheered their Treasurer at the news of more revenue, the Treasurer did not bother to tout any 'health' benefit from further taxing tobacco. Few will cease smoking as a result of the new taxes because these come on top of many others, and follow decades of programs to help change the culture of acceptability of tobacco. It seems that taxation follows the fall in smoking rates.

And there are those advocates whose ignorance of public policy is astounding. Dr Margaret Chan, Director-General of the World Health Organization, addressing a world-wide meeting of parliamentarians, berated them to "Get your governments to raise taxes on tobacco products ... Above all, fight against tax policies ... that punish the poor."[87] It is impossible to use tax policy to cut the demand for tobacco products and not punish the poor, who

---

[86] Delivered on 3 May 2016 on the second reading of the *Appropriation Bill (No. 1) 2016-17* by the Honourable Scott Morrison MP, Treasurer of the Commonwealth of Australia.

[87] Address at the 133rd Inter-Parliamentary Union Assembly Geneva, Switzerland, 19 October 2015.

are their greatest consumers. Even a sure fire sin, such as tobacco consumption, has activists and regulators making errors, and governments gouging.

Tax is not cost free

Most taxes result in some loss of economic efficiency as they distort 'usual' economic behaviour. The deadweight loss impact of taxation arises from the reduced incentive effects associated with additional tax. This is because it drives a wedge between prices paid and received for goods and services. This has been estimated to be on average 27.5 cents in the dollar. The Australia's Future Tax System (Henry review, 2009) reported that the marginal welfare losses from major Commonwealth taxes included 24 cents in the dollar for personal tax and 40 cents for company tax. What this means is that for every $1 of personal income tax raised, community welfare is reduced overall by 24 cents. Likewise, for every $1 of company tax raised, community welfare is reduced overall by 40 cents.[88]

Using the same logic and similar figures, Henry Ergas queried an estimate by the Grattan Institute of the costs of obesity shifted onto others (featured in the next chapter). Over half of the estimated $5.3 billion a year arose from the loss of tax revenue owing to the lower earnings of people who are obese. But, as Ergas pointed out, the cost to the community of reducing tax revenues by a dollar is not one dollar: it is, at most, that dollar's 'opportunity cost', which can be estimated as the economic damage caused by raising another dollar to replace it, with the rest of the fiscal loss being a transfer from one part of the community to another. "On the report's assumptions, that net cost amounts to 25 cents. However, the report not only counts the 25 cents, but also adds to it the original dollar –

---

[88]   ACIL Allen, 2014. *Counting the Costs of Alcohol Policy-relevant Costs to Australia*, 30.

so that 25 cents in community costs becomes $1.25. The estimates of third party costs are egregiously overestimated."[89]

Taxation can recoup spillover costs

Smokers sometimes impose costs on others. The costs of passive smoking, for example, include the costs of disease and premature death caused by passive smoking, as well as the discomfort of those exposed to the smoke of others. A recent assessment concluded that second-hand smoke caused the deaths of 149 Australians in 2004-05.[90] Babies of Australian women who smoke during pregnancy are twice as likely as other babies to have low birth weight and are more likely to require special care.[91] The Henry review, however, indicated that the social costs of tobacco consumption were low compared to the private costs: "Spillover costs need to be taken into account but are small compared with the costs borne by smokers themselves."[92] Taxation to recover the costs of smokers imposed directly on others should, therefore, be small.

The Henry review also considered that in any given year, a smoker's healthcare is likely to cost more on average than that of a non-smoker of the same age and sex. It also thought that because smokers tend to die earlier than non-smokers, the lifetime healthcare costs of smokers and non-smokers in high-income countries might be fairly similar.[93] Unfortunately, the review did not calculate actual health costs throughout a lifetime, or the cost of pensions to the long-lived non-smoker which, as was reported in the previous chapter, are a crucial part of the public health advocate's armoury.

---

[89] Ergas 2016. In a letter to the editor (*The Weekend Australian* 24-25 December 2016), the author of the Grattan report denies the Ergas critique of 'double counting'.

[90] David Collins and Helen Lapsley, 2008. The costs of tobacco, alcohol and illicit drug abuse to Australian society in 2004-05. Department of Health and Ageing. *Monograph Series no. 64*, 53.

[91] Paula Laws et al, 2006. Smoking and pregnancy. *Australian Institute of Health and Welfare, National Perinatal Statistics Unit* No. 33, x.

[92] Australia's Future Tax System, 2009. *Final Report*. Part 2, chapter, e6-3.

[93] Australia's Future Tax System 2009, e6-1.

Or, be an excuse to gouge ...

In his submission to a parliamentary inquiry, Sinclair Davidson questioned the Henry review's acknowledgment of low spillover costs and support for higher taxation.[94] Davidson distinguished two forms of taxation. Because tobacco demand is relatively unaffected by taxation, simple revenue raising could be a straight forward exercise, that is, seeking no change to behaviour.

Alternatively, taxation could be used to discourage tobacco consumption. In the latter, the government wishes to impose a different set of preferences on those freely chosen by smokers. Davidson points out that this strategy risks destroying "consumer utility" and can cause adverse behaviour, and costs, such as a black market in illicit cigarettes. Estimates of the size vary widely, but confirm the existence of an illicit market for tobacco in Australia.[95]

The Henry review considered that Australia's tobacco taxes were modest compared to OECD countries. Davidson, however, demonstrated that excise in Australia was well above a world average on an excise as a percentage of cigarette prices measure and that Australian excise, at the time of his submission, comprised 60 per cent of the price.[96]

A second element of the critique consisted of assumptions about the inferred behaviour of smokers. This is an argument about how governments should intervene in markets where consumers fail to understand their own preferences because of, for example, a lack of knowledge of the product and its health effects. The review examined the extent to which smokers value the present over the future, and the extent to which smokers can be described as being

---

[94] Sinclair Davidson, 2016. *Submission to Parliamentary Joint Committee on Law Enforcement Inquiry into Illicit Tobacco.* Australian Parliament, 11.
[95] The Cancer Council of Australia, *Tobacco in Australia: Facts and Issues.* 10.9.
[96] Davidson 2016, 6.

'sophisticated' or 'naïve'. Sophisticated smokers understand that their future selves might wish to quit smoking and act consistently with that objective, while naïve smokers under-estimate the preferences of their future selves. In order to justify its recommendation for a "substantial increase" in tobacco excise the Henry review would have to demonstrate that Australian smokers are both naïve and value the present substantially over the future.

Using the Henry review estimates, Davidson found that excise rates were (then) high enough to force even naïve smokers to value the future and not the present (they were not being irrational by consuming tobacco in the present). Davidson concluded that there was no 'market failure' to justify government intervention, and no "basis to argue that tobacco excise should be substantially increased – merely the anti-tobacco prejudice of the Review itself."[97] Davidson's critique was that the basis for government intervention was not revenue maximisation or social cost minimisation but, rather, paternalistic.

Figure 3. Smoking rates and tobacco control, Australia

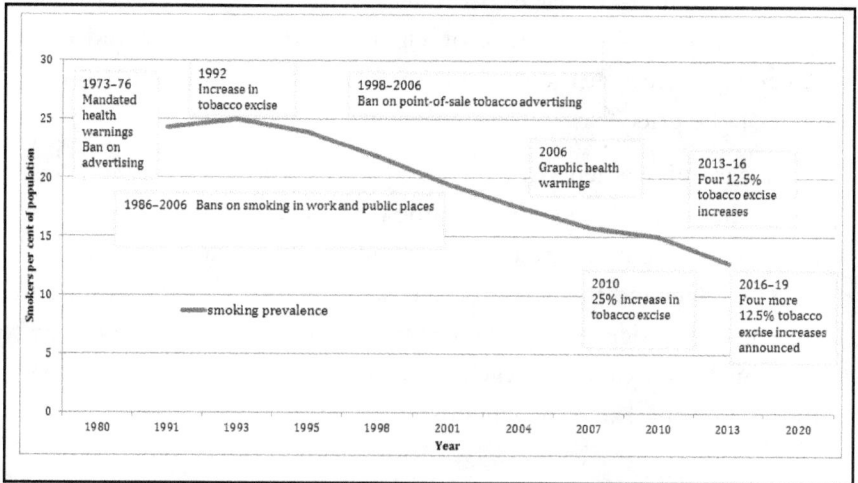

Source: Australian Government, Department of Health, 2016. http://www.health.gov. au/internet/main/publishing.nsf/Content/tobacco-kff accessed 4 August 2016.

[97]   Davidson 2016, 8.

Figure 3 tracks the decline of smoking prevalence rates (14 years and over) in Australia from 1990 to 2013, and the important policy initiatives, prior, and during the period. Smoking prevalence rates in the last two decades have declined substantially. Tobacco control measures implemented in Australia suggest the measures have had a substantial impact on the decline. They also suggest that a 'cultural revolution' based on better information, advertising bans (combat 'presence of mind' temptations) and inconvenience (banning indoor smoking) have been key measures. Tax increases appear to have come at the end of the culture change, after prevalence rates had dived from 25 per cent in 1991 to 13 per cent in 2013.

And yet, in 2013, legislation was passed for four further increases in tobacco taxation. Excise rates for tobacco increased by 12.5 per cent 2013-16[98] and, at its 2016-17 Budget, the Australian Government announced a further four annual 12.5 per cent increases in tobacco excise.[99] The Treasurer did not make any pretence of a health dividend; the health argument simply provided a convenient cover for extra revenue. Davidson's accusation of paternalism seems correct, and there is also a large dose of gouging.

Or, makes little difference ...

Taxes are unlikely to be an effective way of reducing the costs of other sin products, such as problem gambling. The Henry review had the following observations on taxation and problem gambling.

> To the extent that existing gambling taxes recoup costs imposed on others they do not affect the odds that gamblers face. But even when taxes do more than recoup 'economic rent', they can only mitigate the effects of problem gambling if they increase the average amount lost by a player per dollar bet, and if problem

[98] Australian Taxation Office, https://www.ato.gov.au/Business/Excise-and-excise-equivalent-goods/Tobacco-excise/Excise-rates-for-tobacco/

[99] see above, Morrison 2016.

gamblers respond by reducing their losses.

The price of gambling for some games, such as many casino table games, is fixed by the rules of the game and will not be affected by gambling taxes (although businesses may be able to adjust the price by providing discounts of various types or making adjustments to the rules). In other games, such as TAB wagering, the price of gambling (the average player loss) may be affected by gambling taxes but is not immediately apparent to the gambler. In such cases, increasing the price of gambling is not likely to affect the behaviour of problem gamblers.

Even where the price of gambling is affected by gambling taxes and is apparent to the gambler, problem gamblers may not markedly reduce their losses. If their gambling is constrained only by the amount of money available to them, their losses will not fall. If they face other constraints on their gambling, like the amount of time they can devote to gambling, higher prices may lead to higher losses and more severe problems.[100]

Approximately one per cent of the adult population are problem gamblers, so using taxes to help counteract problem gambling imposes high costs on the large majority of non-problem gamblers. Other policy interventions may help to address spillover costs and the costs borne by gamblers themselves. These interventions, some of which have been implemented in Australia, include limiting or prohibiting the advertising of gambling services.[101] None of the above has stopped government from taxing gamblers. The most recent imposition in South Australia is an attempt to keep some taxation in South Australia from Internet gambling.

The 2016-17 State Budget introduced in South Australia a "place of consumption tax" of 15 per cent on the net wagering revenue of betting companies offering services to South Australia, effective

---

[100] Australia's Future Tax System 2009, *E7–2*.

[101] Gary Banks, 2011. Evidence and social policy: the case of gambling. *Presentation to South Australian Centre for Economic Studies, Corporate Seminar*, Adelaide, 30 March.

from 1 July 2017. All bets placed in South Australia with Australian-based betting companies will be liable for the tax. South Australia will be the first Australian jurisdiction to introduce a wagering tax based on the place of consumption. The place of consumption tax will apply to bets on horse, harness and greyhound racing, and bets on sports such as AFL, cricket and soccer. It will also apply to other bets, such as those on the winner of the federal election or the Academy Awards.[102] Presumably these taxes have the potential to drive gambling to offshore sites.

Or, keep the public health lobby quiet …

There is an expectation among anti-gambling public health campaigners that a great deal of revenue raised should be devoted to prevention. The logic is somewhat twisted as the tax is often touted as lowering the risk of harm, in other words, the tax is the program. And/or, the tax is sufficient to recoup spillover costs, including costs of the sinner shared by others. Whether taxes are the solution, or recoup spillover costs, or simply raise funds, is in practice difficult to determine. These monies should probably return to general revenue. Nevertheless, governments respond to lobbies, so it is often the case that some monies are diverted to specific programs of prevention and rehabilitation.

Gambling taxes constituted 6.5 per cent of all state revenue in 2014-15, almost $5 billion.[103] State governments allocate part of gambling revenue to social programs such as problem gambling services and research into the impact of gambling on the community. In some states, substantial amounts of revenue are allocated to health services. In Victoria, for example, more than $1 billion per

---

[102]   Revenue South Australia, *Wagering tax announcement*. 7 July 2016.
[103]   Australian Bureau of Statistics, 2016. *Taxation Revenue Australia 2014-15*. Table 18 Taxation total all states, state and local government.

year from gambling revenue is allocated to various social programs: the Community Support Fund, the Hospitals and Charities Fund and the Mental Health Fund.[104] The SA wagering tax, for example, is expected to raise $9.2 million each year in new revenue. Of that, $500 000 will be contributed annually to the Gamblers Rehabilitation Fund. This will be the first time that the betting industry has contributed to the Gamblers Rehabilitation Fund.

The US Master Settlement Agreement, whereby tobacco companies agreed to pay annual sums of money to the states to compensate them for health-care costs related to smoking (a minimum of US$206 billion over the first twenty-five years), created and funded the National Public Education Foundation. The Foundation is dedicated to reducing youth smoking and preventing diseases associated with smoking. [105] There is considerable complaint, however, that those monies have not been sufficiently targeted towards prevention. From 2000 to 2009, the states have received US$79 billion from the tobacco settlement (and US$124 billion from tobacco taxes). During this time, the states have allocated US$6.5 billion to tobacco prevention and cessation programs.[106]

Taxation can be costly, punitive, and ineffective as a means of 'solving' public health problems. It is as well to check which taxes are doing good and which are exercises in gouging. Public health advocates do not help the cause by proclaiming the effectiveness of taxation and seeking to divert its income stream to their cause, of which taxation was meant to be a solution.

---

[104] Victorian State Government Department of Treasury and Finance, *Community Support Fund*.

[105] Kathleen Michon, 2015. Tobacco litigation: history and recent developments. *NOLO* 30 December. http://www.nolo.com/legal-encyclopedia/tobacco-litigation-history-and-development-32202.html accessed 28 February 2017.

[106] Campaign for Tobacco-Free Kids, 2008. A decade of broken promises: the 1998 state tobacco settlement ten years later. *Robert Wood Johnson Foundation*, i.

6

Taxation is ineffective where the source of harm is diffuse

We estimate about 10 per cent of Australia's obesity problem is due to ... sugar-sweetened beverages.[107]

-- Grattan Institute

Okay, Grattan Institute, so why recommend an excise tax on "non-alcoholic, water-based beverages that contain added sugar", knowing that sugar is a single nutrient and obesity is caused by excess calories from any nutrient? Sugar can weaken appetite control and lead to increases in weight gain and greater risk of obesity,[108] and sugar is added to an enormous array of processed foods, but taxing one source of one element of obesity-creating-foods might not do much good.

Tax on junk food, or one element of it, to reduce consumption is more complex than taxing tobacco or alcohol, and unlike those products, there is no absolutely agreed definition of what constitutes healthy or harmful food. As a result, "it has been relatively easy for opponents of taxation to argue against having differential taxation rates for different food types. The implementation of food taxes in 'real life' settings is limited and the analysis of the effectiveness of these is even more limited."[109] So say public health advocates. But,

---

[107] Stephen Duckett and Hal Swerissen, 2016. *A Sugary Drinks Tax: Recovering the Community Costs of Obesity.* Melbourne: Grattan Institute.

[108] World Health Organization, 2003. *Technical Report Series. Diet, Nutrition and the Prevention of Chronic Diseases.* Geneva: WHO, 916.

[109] Tracy Comans et al, 2013. The cost-effectiveness and consumer acceptability of taxation strategies to reduce rates of overweight and obesity among children in Australia: study protocol. *BMC Public Health* 13(1182), 4.

they are mistaken; there is sufficient evidence in real life settings to suggest that a sugar tax or, indeed, other food taxes, is not a useful tool to combat obesity.

Are sugar-sweetened beverages a major contributor to obesity?

The world-wide increase in obesity and related chronic diseases has largely been driven by "Nutritional transitions in low-income and middle-income countries [that] are typically characterized by increases in the consumption of animal fat and protein, refined grains, and added sugar."[110] As these researchers note, obesity is multi-faceted. Sugar is but one source of energy and sugary drinks but one source of sugar. The majority of free sugars consumed in Australia, for example, are from the energy-dense, nutrient-poor 'discretionary' foods and beverages. Just over half (52 per cent) of free sugars in the diet are consumed from beverages, with the leading beverages being soft drinks, sports and energy drinks (19 per cent), fruit and vegetable juices and drinks (13 per cent) and cordial (4.9 per cent). The leading foods are confectionary and cakes/muffins (each contributing 8.7 per cent).[111]

Meanwhile, there is evidence in Australia that while obesity's incidence has increased, overall the proportion of people aged two years and over that consumed sweetened beverages decreased from 49 per cent in 1995 to 42 per cent in 2011-12. This was driven primarily by a decrease in consumption of cordial, with a decrease in consumption among children from 35 per cent in 1995 to 11 per cent in 2011-12. The greatest decreases in consumption of sweetened beverages were

---

[110] V.S. Malik et al, 2013. Global obesity: trends, risk factors and policy implications. *National Review of Endocrinology* 9(1), 13.

[111] Australian Bureau of Statistics, 2016. *Australian Health Survey: Consumption of Added Sugars 2011-12*, 6.

seen among children, with the proportion of children aged 2-3 years who consumed sweetened beverages decreasing by more than half (67 per cent compared with 31 per cent).[112]

And, just as there has been no inoculation for tobacco (although nicotine substitutes help), or for alcohol, neither is there for food. 'Big Pharma' may not be able to come to the rescue. Pharmacotherapy for obesity has witnessed several promising drugs but these were eventually withdrawn because of unacceptable safety concerns. Until recently, there have been few 'well-tolerated' medications available for effective management of obesity. While scientists remain optimistic there are new medications in the pipeline, and it is anticipated that the pharmaceutical "gap in treatment options" will improve, there is only the hope of "adding to the possibilities for bespoke weight loss programmes."[113]

How many lives would be saved?

A recent paper estimated the consequences of an additional 20 per cent tax on sugar-sweetened beverages on health and health care expenditure in Australia. The researchers were keen to show that the tax would generate an estimated $400 million in revenue each year. The major consequence on health, however, was that an estimated 1606 extra people would be alive as a result of the tax.[114] Given that at least 3.7 million Australians will die in the next 25 years, 1606 seems a very small return on a considerable taxation measure.[115] Indeed,

---

[112] Australian Bureau of Statistics, 2014. *Australian Health Survey: Nutrition First Results: Foods and Nutrients, 2011-12.*

[113] K. Fujioka, 2015. Current and emerging medications for overweight or obesity in people with comorbidities. *Diabetes, Obesity and Metabolism* 17, 1029.

[114] Veerman et al, 2016.

[115] There were 147,678 deaths in 2013, so a crude measure of 25 multiplied by that number could underestimate the rate. Australian Institute of Health and Welfare, http://www.aihw.gov.au/deaths/ accessed 26 October 2016.

Australia has had a de facto sugar tax since 2000 with the introduction of the Goods and Services Tax, which taxes processed foods, leaving fresh foods untaxed. All the while, obesity has increased.

A United States case study on sugar tax provides little comfort to sugar tax proponents. Nearly two-thirds of all states currently tax soft drinks using excise taxes or sales taxes. An analysis of the impact of changes in states' taxation rates from 1990 to 2006 on changes in body mass (BMI) and obesity suggested that weight does respond to changes in soft drink tax rates, but not by much. An increase of one percentage point in the state soft drink tax rate led to a decrease in BMI of 0.003 points. Extrapolating, the results suggested that increasing the soft drink tax to 58 per cent would decrease the mean BMI in the United States by 0.16 points. In comparison, the average gain in BMI between 1990 and 2006 was more than 2.3 points. Increasing the tax rate comparable to that of cigarettes yielded a decrease in the proportion of the population who are obese or overweight by nearly 0.7 percentage points. The conclusion: "although increasing the tax rate on soft drinks to be comparable with cigarettes will not halt the obesity epidemic, the impact on population weight would likely be non-negligible."[116] This is not a lot to look forward to.

The Danish fat tax

To the lack of impact on health, there are additional problems associated with any food tax. A number were experienced with the recent brief experiment with a fat tax in Denmark. In October 2011, Denmark introduced the world's first fat tax. The tax included meat, dairy, animal fat, oils, margarine and butter blends as well as composed foods containing these products. The taxation rate was DKK 16 per kg of saturated fat excluding 25 per cent value added tax. A threshold

---

[116] Jason Fletcher et al, 2010. Can soft drink taxes reduce population weight? *Contemporary Economic Policy* 28(1), 24.

limit of 2.3 per cent saturated fat exempted all types of regular drinking milk and milk-based yoghurts. The tax was imposed on anyone producing or importing foodstuffs for commercial purposes and was expected to be passed at consumer prices in retail outlets, restaurants, and fast food outlets.

Research on the tax concluded that Denmark's 'fat tax' proved economically damaging and did not change the habits of 80 per cent of Danes. The tax led to a tiny 0.4 per cent reduction in fat consumption in seven months, while food prices increased by 14 per cent. The tax led to some strange behaviour on purchases. The sale of butter blends and margarine decreased, while the sale of butter, oils, cream, chips and snacks increased. Decreasing sales of cookies and biscuits combined with increasing sales of chips and snacks indicates a tendency for consumers to have shifted from sweet to salty types of between-meal foods during the fat tax.

In addition, a tax that specifically targets saturated fat can lead to a simultaneous reduction in the intake of unsaturated fat, since some of those foods high in saturated fat are also high in unsaturated fat, e.g. butter blends and margarine, which can potentially outweigh the positive health benefits of a tax on saturated fat. The changes in consumption patterns caused by the fat tax, therefore, had only a marginal effect on the risk to the population of ischaemic heart disease.

The avowedly pro-fat tax researchers pressed on, concluding, "governments should implement higher taxation rates in order for food taxes to have the intended health effects. This, however, involves a risk of increasing economic inequalities, as food taxes are regressive, i.e. burden low-income households proportionately more than high-income households."[117] To compensate, researchers suggest a tax-subsidy, and hope that politicians do not use food taxes to generate

---

[117] Malene Bødker et al, 2015(a). The Danish fat tax: effects on consumption patterns and risk of ischaemic heart disease. *Preventive Medicine* 77, 203.

revenue.[118] But, would the poor spend the subsidy on junk food? The problems associated with the Danish fat tax: economic damage, lack of effect on people's health, increased economic inequality and government gouging may not deter public health advocates, but they certainly turned off everyone else. It was repealed in January 2013 after only 15 months.[119]

Inequality exacerbated

A recent small sample study of 160 French women simulated the effect of a five per cent value added tax on 22 food items. The study concluded that a fat-tax policy is unsuitable for substantially affecting the nutrients purchased by French households, and leads to 'ambiguous' effects. Although it would generate large tax revenue, the fat tax is extremely regressive.

Somewhat bizarrely, the researchers were more interested in health inequality that any health benefit, a further insight into the minds of some advocates, particularly in Europe. For example, attempts to improve the health of the overall population may "increase health disparities between social groups because those who were formerly at a lower risk of exposure derive more benefits than those who were formerly at a greater exposure to risk."[120] The researchers thought that this was a serious problem, not that some were harmed, but that not everyone benefited. This is quite different to, for example, a tax that punishes the poor and has little effect on health.

The study suggested that food price policies, for example, fruit and vegetable subsidies and food tax combined with appropriate subsidies, might improve some aspects of diet quality. Limited dietary changes

---

[118] M Bødker et al, 2015(b). The rise and fall of the world's first fat tax. *Health Policy* 119, 737.

[119] Bødker 2015(b), 737.

[120] Nicole Darmon et al, 2014. Food price policies improve diet quality while increasing socioeconomic inequalities in nutrition. *The International Journal of Behavioral Nutrition and Physical Activity* 11(1), 66.

were, however, only obtained by price changes of 30 per cent. As the researchers admitted, "it is unlikely that actual policies would use such high rates, which could be judged politically unacceptable."[121]

To achieve modest gains in health among the poor, not only would there be riots in the streets over 30 per cent price rises, and subsidies on designated foods which they apparently do not favour, there might also be a response from the food industry to hold on to the market for their goods. The food industry might respond to tax changes by, for example, changing the nutritional quality of the taxed products. It might modify the composition of the taxed products by substituting more expensive components and/or implementing new processes, making the modified product less affordable. It might cause some shifts in demand from high-end supermarkets towards low-end discount stores – a shift that seems to have been utilised by discount chains to raise the prices of butter and margarine by more than the pure tax increase.[122]

Taxation would be followed by regulation in a merry-go-round of increased imposition and surveillance. The strategies may aggravate class disparities in the nutritional quality of food chosen. Heaven forbid, a fat tax might have perverse effects in so far as it could "exacerbate nutritional disparities among consumers"![123]

Substitution

While the public health lobby do their best to change the consumption habits of the recalcitrant consumer, the consumer constantly undermines their plans. A US study combined soft drink tax data

---

[121] Darmon at al 2014, 66.

[122] Jørgen Dejgård Jensen and Sinne Smed, 2013. The Danish tax on saturated fat: short run effects on consumption, substitution patterns and consumer prices of fats. *Food Policy* 42, 26.

[123] Olivier Allais et al, 2010. The effects of a fat tax on French households' purchases: a nutritional approach. *American Journal of Agricultural Economics* 92(1), 243.

between 1989 and 2006 with the National Health Examination and Nutrition Survey in order to examine the effects of soft drink taxes on child and adolescent soft drink consumption, substitution patterns, and weight outcomes. Overall, the study found evidence of moderate reductions in soft drink consumption from current soda tax rates but it also found that reductions in calories from soda were completely offset by increases in calories from other beverages. Therefore, "soda taxes do not reduce weight in children and adolescents and is, therefore, likely an ineffective obesity tax".[124]

In apparently more controlled situations such as schools, substitution looms as the impediment to change of behaviour. In the 2011-12 school year, school food services in a district of Oregon, USA, removed chocolate milk in kindergarten to grade five and offered skim milk instead. The reasoning was that chocolate milk could have up to twice as much sugar as white milk. Removing chocolate milk from school cafeterias may, therefore, reduce childhood obesity. Milk, however, has nutrients essential for bone growth and development, so that, in that regard, any milk is better than no milk. A study of the effect of removing chocolate milk had astounding results. Among these schools, eliminating chocolate milk was associated with a 10 per cent decrease in average daily milk sales, a 10 per cent increase in the cost of milk consumption, and a 30 per cent increase in milk waste.[125]

In addition to these potentially harmful changes to selection, the researchers asked whether changing the availability of chocolate milk influenced other behaviours such as within-meal compensation or after-school snacking or decreased lunch sales. The research did not study whether students compensated at lunch, or after school, by consuming higher calorie beverages or snacks, but they were very

[124] Jason Fletcher et al, 2010. The effects of soft drink taxes on child and adolescent consumption and weight outcomes. *Journal of Public Economics* 94, 968.
[125] Andrew Hanks et al, 2014. Chocolate milk consequences: a pilot study evaluating the consequences of banning chocolate milk in school cafeterias. *PLOS ONE* 9(4), 1.

suspicious that that might be the case. They concluded, "drinking chocolate milk is better than drinking an alternative caloric drink, such as a sports drink, or even not eating a school lunch."[126]

Consumers do change their habits when goods are taxed. Taxes on sugary drinks can slow their purchase, but not slow growth in waistlines. Some studies suggest that substitutions and compensation might occur that moderate any effect on consumption, but there is considerable variation.[127]

The following fascinating study tried to unravel the extent to which consumers switch under a new tax.[128]

From Coke to Coors

> Could taxation of calorie-dense foods such as soft drinks be used to reduce obesity?
>
> A six-month field experiment was conducted in an American city of 62,000 where half of the 113 households recruited into the study faced a 10 per cent tax on calorie-dense foods and beverages and half did not.
>
> The tax resulted in a short-term (1-month) decrease in soft drink purchases, but no decrease over a 3-month or 6-month period. Moreover, in beer-purchasing households, this tax led to increased purchases of beer.
>
> Consistent with the previous literature, the evidence suggested that consumers engaged in substitution as a result of specific food taxes. Specifically, households that frequently bought beer bought even more beer, and households that frequently bought soft drinks purchased even more. The tax triggered sales of water, but any health benefit were completely overridden by the additional calories purchased through soft drinks.
>
> Taxes on less healthy foods may not succeed in reducing soft drink consumption or in reducing calorie consumption. Of greater concern is that such a tax may encourage an increased consumption of alcohol among some households.[129]

---

[126] Hanks 2014, 1.

[127] There is some propensity for like with like substitution, bad or good substitution. See Zhen Miao et al, 2013. Accounting for product substitution in the analysis of food taxes targeting obesity. *Health Economics* 22, 1318-1343.

[128] Andrew Hanks et al, 2013. From Coke to Coors: a field study of a fat tax and its unintended consequences. *Journal of Nutrition Education and Behaviour* 45(4), Supplement, July-August, S40, 26.

[129] Hanks 2013, S40.

We know that consumers will shift their demand toward cheaper foods in response to fat taxes. Taxing sugary drinks will certainly reduce their consumption, but it is likely to increase consumption of very close substitutes such as diet soft drinks, and also fruit and vegetable juices, milk, water, and maybe alcoholic beverages. Such a tax might also increase demand for a complementary good like salty snacks. The net impact of a sugary drink tax on obesity therefore depends not only on the price responsiveness of the demand for such drinks, but also on the responsiveness of the demand for a broad range of substitutes and complements.

The net effect on calorie intake of this shifting is not guaranteed to be negative because consumers choose foods based on many characteristics beyond caloric content. Indeed, some taxes on some types of food might even raise obesity if close substitutes actually have higher caloric content.[130] The Grattan Institute will have to return to the drawing board.

---

[130] Ryan Edwards, 2011. Commentary: soda taxes, obesity, and the shifty behavior of consumers. *Preventive Medicine* 52(6), 417.

7

Estimating the cost of harm can be a fool's errand

Australia's largest non-profit provider of health and aged care services has called on the Coalition, Labor and the Greens to sign-up to reducing alcohol-related illness and injury in Australia by 20 per cent by 2025.[131]

-- St Vincent's Health Australia

Okay, so St Vincent's called on political parties to sign up to a target to reduce alcohol-related illness by 20 per cent. St Vincent's has been in the field helping alcoholics and others since 1964, so you can see that they might be sick of it. Perhaps that is why they want to bring it all to a head in a national policy. They want to do this knowing that just 3.4 per cent of drinkers are in the 'harmful' category.[132] They want to do this also knowing that there has been a decline in per capita consumption of alcohol in Australia since 1960.[133]

Some of their policy is targeted and traditional, for example, "treatment services for people with alcohol dependence," but most applies to almost everyone. In shades of tobacco regulation, St Vincent's wants an end to all alcohol advertising and sponsorship, alcohol to be taxed on the basis of alcohol content/greatest level of harm (volumetric tax), pictorial health warnings and a host of limitations on trading hours.[134]

---

[131] St Vincent's Health Australia, 2016. *Restoring the Balance: A New Approach to Alcohol in Australia.* Melbourne: St. Vincent's Health Australia.

[132] Six standard drinks per day. Marsden Jacob 2015, 13.

[133] Australian Bureau of Statistics, 2015. *Apparent Consumption of Alcohol, Australia, 2013-14.*

[134] St Vincent's Health Australia 2016, 15.

There are two big issues that politicians need to confront before they do St Vincent's bidding. If it is possible to recover the costs of alcohol harm caused by drinkers that spillover to others, who else has to pay, and how much? Is it possible to diminish the amount of harm without stopping other's enjoyment? As one researcher eloquently stated, "How much pleasure should be foregone among those who drink moderately to dissuade those who over-indulge?"[135] This is the stuff of all harm regulation, played out in excruciating detail, particularly in the taxation of alcohol.

Poorly targeted

If all you have is a hammer, you treat every problem as a nail.[136] Economist's, and public health activist's, hammer is taxation. If tax on alcohol could be targeted at that 'one drink too many', it may have the effect of stopping harmful consumption, or at least, raise money to cover the cost of harm from those who offend. In the real world, it is not possible to put a charge on every drink over and above what someone deems 'one drink too many'. As a result, taxes on alcohol are levied on all alcohol products, the effect of which is to raise the cost of drinking to all drinkers. This makes tax a blunt instrument for reducing the spillover costs of alcohol use. It means that consumers who enjoy alcohol responsibly face an unnecessarily high price (pay too much tax). Even though tax on alcohol raises revenue for government, it is not a costless way of addressing alcohol abuse. As with all policy interventions, the benefits of taxation should be weighed against the costs.[137]

A recent study based on Australian National Drug Strategy

---

[135] Joshua Byrnes et al, 2013. Can harms associated with high-intensity drinking be reduced by increasing the price of alcohol? *Drug and Alcohol Review* 32(1), 27-30.

[136] Maslow's law of the instrument. Abraham Maslow, 1966. *The Psychology of Science*, Maurice Bassett Publishing, 15.

[137] Australia's Future Tax System 2009, *E5–1*.

Household Surveys tried to work out who changed their drinking and by how much after price (tax) increases.[138] The results suggest that Australian drinkers reduced their overall level of alcohol consumption in response to price increases mostly by increasing the number of occasions on which they do not drink at all and by decreasing the number of occasions of low-intensity drinking. They did not significantly reduce their frequency of moderate- and high-intensity drinking.

In other words, price increases seem unlikely to have significantly reduced the number of occasions on which people drink at higher intensities (5-9 and 10 or more standard drinks). So, those for whom drinking is a pleasure and does little harm were forced to change their habits and those who drank a lot, and were more likely to do harm, changed little.

Price rises were not only ineffective in slowing problem drinkers, the authors noted that respondents to the survey may have under-reported their levels of drinking, which could undermine the accuracy with which price actually influenced demand at each level of intensity. Price rises may also have been ineffective because retailers may respond to price increases with short-term discounting, or drinkers may shift consumption from pubs to take-away.

To emphasise the point, the authors of the study recommend "complementary legislation, such as earlier closing times for venues that sell alcohol", to curb the frequency of high-intensity consumption.[139] State governments have been wrestling with this side of alcohol policy for generations.[140]

---

[138] Self-reported patterns of alcohol consumption and demographic data, Australian National Drug Strategy Household Surveys, conducted in 2001, 2004 and 2007, comprising a total of 79 545 respondents. Byrnes 2013, 27.

[139] Byrnes 2013, 30.

[140] New South Wales Auditor-General's Report Performance Audit, 2013. *Cost of Alcohol Abuse to the NSW Government*, 2.

When too much tax is never enough

The Foundation for Alcohol Research and Education paid economists Marsden Jacobs to estimate the optimal rate for social benefit of alcohol taxation in Australia. To do so, they had to estimate costs and benefits of alcohol consumption. Estimates of the annual social costs for Australia range from $3.8 billion to $36 billion. Incidentally, St Vincent's used a figure of $20 billion. The differences in calculated social costs reflect different views about which costs should be counted and how they should be counted.

In calculating the costs and benefits of alcohol consumption at a given price, fine judgments need to be made about the 'rationality' of drinkers. Marsden Jacobs, sensibly, used two scenarios, one where heavy drinkers derived benefits from excessive consumption, and another where they derived only a portion of the benefit. Under the assumption that there was no loss of benefit for heavy drinkers from an increase in excise rates, the rate of excise increase that would maximise net benefits to society was measured at 145 per cent. Such an increase would deliver $688 million per year in net benefits. This policy would result in an annual increase in excise and tax revenue to the Commonwealth government of $6.6 billion.

When they relaxed the assumption that harmful levels of alcohol consumption had no benefit to consumers, the rate of excise increase that would maximise net benefits to society was 74 per cent, yielding $207 million per year in net benefits. This change of policy would result in an annual increase in excise and tax revenue of to the Commonwealth government of $4.3 billion.

These numbers look impressive, net benefits overall, taking into account loss of satisfaction from moderate drinkers and decline in some harms associated with alcohol. But was it realistic? The answer, given by the economists, was a startling no. In careful language they concluded, "the percentage increases in excise rates that are found to maximise net benefits to society are well above any changes that have been observed in practice."[141] In other words, these rates of increase in excise are not plausible.

The analysis has a number of additional limitations and weaknesses readily acknowledged by the authors. First the analysis has not modelled the possibility that consumers of alcohol, might switch to other substances, such as illicit drugs, in response to a price change in alcohol. This means that the true costs of higher rates of excise could be understated. Moreover, the largest figure by far in the two scenarios was revenue, not benefits. Of course, there would be a cost in its gathering, and every chance that the monies might not be used sensibly.

Building momentous numbers

In Jonathan Pincus's term, the 'momentous' numbers preferred by public health advocates to provide an excuse to control each person's consumption decisions are arrived at by various means. There is disagreement about measuring the cost of the use and misuse of alcohol, and about the costs that are private and the costs that are spillover (non-private). Some researchers have identified and measured community expenditures and losses that are proportional to alcohol misuse – including some costs borne by the drinker. This approach has tended to result in a relatively large estimate of social costs. Other researchers have excluded costs borne by private individuals. This approach has tended to treat many costs as private leaving a smaller estimate of social costs.

A further distinction between private and spillover costs is that between tangible and intangible costs of alcohol misuse. The discrepancy in costs estimates between studies is largely a result of

---

[141] Marsden Jacob 2015, 20.

whether intangible costs are included. Tangible costs from alcohol misuse and its consequences include medical services and hospital-related costs. Intangible costs from alcohol misuse include effects on the health and quality of life of the drinker and family members of the drinker. The Marsden Jacob study explicitly excluded intangible costs from cost of alcohol misuse because of the uncertainty of the estimates. Where this is the case, the subsequent costs estimate has been qualified as being a minimal cost to society as a result of alcohol misuse.

To cap off debate around the costs of the effects of alcohol and what should be counted and how costs are assigned is the all too common error by the public health lobby: a failure to calculate consumer surpluses,

> *So it is a mystery how the researchers felt able to draw their conclusions about the effects of a minimum alcohol price on health, crime, absentee rates and so on. If they do not know by how much a minimum alcohol price will increase the consumption of DIY alcohol, illegal drugs, glue fumes and the rest, they cannot know its effects on public health, crime and employment.*[142]

Building momentous numbers is a big part of the lobby's toolkit. Another is to leap to solutions, without knowing their costs and impact.

Policy-relevant spillover costs

An ACIL Allen discussion paper focused on determining the degree to which public policy measures can reduce the spillover costs of alcohol, whatever they may be. As the paper argues, the importance of being able to understand the degree to which different public policy measures can reduce costs "have been somewhat lost as a

---

[142] Jamie Whyte, 2013. *Quack Policy Abusing Science in the Cause of Paternalism*. London: The Institute of Economic Affairs, 25.

result of the controversy surrounding the magnitude of the different costs estimates."[143]

While spillover costs comprise all costs imposed on persons external to a drinker arising from their consumption of alcohol (externalities) and non-internalised costs to the drinker, policy-relevant spillover costs comprise only those spillover costs that can be affected by public policy interventions. Policy-relevant spillover costs do not include private costs to the individual from alcohol misuse.

ACIL Allen argue that policy-relevant spillover costs should be defined in a way that assists in answering the following questions:

- What impacts are relevant as a basis for possible government intervention in decisions to consume alcohol?
- What are the relevant policy costs and how do they differ by the severity of alcohol misuse?
- What avoidable costs are amenable to public policy initiatives and behaviour change?
- What costs can be addressed by public policy measures?
- What public policy interventions best mitigate the policy-relevant costs from alcohol misuse?[144]

These are sensible questions, the answers to which may cause public health advocates to be wary about generating momentous numbers used to prejudge a rush into taxation and regulation as the cure for the ills of alcohol among some small number of people.

It might be worth conceiving the problem in quite different terms.

---

143   ACIL Allen 2014, 4.
144   ACIL Allen 2014, 27.

A different hammer

Public health advocates need to be clear what it is they hope to achieve by their actions. For example, in the case of alcohol, is it to achieve a change to culture, or less alcohol consumption? What if drunken behaviour is culturally determined? Like the decline in smoking, perhaps governments can help to set the terms of understanding, but individuals ultimately determine their choices. As the anthropologist, Anne Fox, has observed, "It is unlikely that we will achieve real and positive change in the drinking culture until we have a better understanding of what is driving it."[145]

Fox observed that as long as alcohol exists no amount of regulation, education, propaganda, restriction, or taxation will deter the 'hard core' of dedicated abusers from periodically (or regularly) exceeding the official maximum 'safe' allowance. For explanation, we must look to the social significance of the substance.[146] In a drinking culture such as the Irish, for example, and in a relatively uniform group such as students, a recent study found a strong family history of drinking habits among the Irish. Parental and sibling drinking affected both actual alcohol consumption and standards for what is considered normal or acceptable drinking behaviour. In addition, however, the culture also operated at regional and national levels, which combined to create "complex deep-rooted cultural and historical factors that facilitate alcohol consumption."[147]

Drunkenness and drunken comportment are most often regarded as being directly proportional to the amount of alcohol consumed. The very same person on the same dose of alcohol, however, can

---

[145] Anne Fox, 2015. Understanding behaviour in the Australian and New Zealand night-time economies: an anthropological study. *Unpublished*, 5.

[146] R Room and K Mäkelä, 2000. Typologies of the cultural position of drinking. *Journal of the Study of Alcohol* 61(3), 475-83.

[147] Liam Delaney et al, 2013. Why do some Irish drink so much? Family, historical and regional effects on students' alcohol consumption and subjective normative thresholds. *Review of Economics of the Household* 11(1), 25.

react in different ways on different occasions and in different settings. This would not happen if the responses were purely physiological. Morphologically similar humans in different cultures react completely differently to being 'under the influence'. Some cultures see very little violence and anti-social behaviour despite similar levels and patterns of consumption to other nations with high levels of such harm.

A recent analysis of all current statistics on both reported and (estimated) unreported alcohol-related assaults in Australia and the estimated number of 'nights out' found that only 0.11 per cent of nights-out result in alcohol-related violence. In other words, 99.89 per cent of drinking occasions remain violence free. If alcohol were a prescribed medication, "a side-effect that was reported in only 0.11 per cent of cases would not be considered to have been caused by the drug."[148] Fox reported that a policewoman confirmed this with an astute observation based on several years of weekend patrols in a major Australian city: "I have never met a violent drunk who was not also violent when sober."[149]

Newcastle was the site of a recent experiment to reduce weekend violence and mayhem. In 2008, a raft of measures were imposed on licensed venues, including earlier closing, lockouts from 1 am, restrictions on the sale of certain drinks, and other measures affecting the management of drinking venues. The police in Newcastle adopted a 'zero- tolerance' approach to misbehaviour in the 'nightlife economy' and imposed heavy, on-the-spot fines for all misdemeanours.

While the results of the Newcastle experiment appear impressive – a reduction in violent incidents from 99 per quarter in the Newcastle CBD before the change to 68 per quarter after – they have not been repeated as successfully in other areas such as Geelong. One reason for this may be that Newcastle police employed another strategy – a dramatic increase in bail compliance checks. As Newcastle police

---

[148] Data Analysis Australia Pty Ltd, 2014. How often does a night out lead to an assault. *Unpublished*, 4.

[149] Fox 2015, 51.

Superintendent John Gralton explained: "five per cent of the population causes 90 per cent of the problem ... Our bail compliance checks have gone from 40 to 400 a month." Every night, police in Newcastle systematically check that offenders who are out on bail or probation and subject to curfew are not out on the street.[150]

Because many people perceive the benefits of drinking to outweigh the harms, Fox argued that alcohol education must refocus on what people perceive to be the benefits and assist them to achieve these (largely social) goals without harming themselves in the process. Young people in particular are focussed on appearing attractive, desirable, socially accepted, confident. They also want to experience pleasure, fun, novelty and excitement in their lives. For many, this is what alcohol provides.

Fox considered that to change a culture of drunken 'disinhibition' requires questioning what is so strongly inhibited in culture that a chemical agent is required to 'loosen it'. In drinking cultures, the message to children is that they cannot relax, be friendly, sociable, loving, helpful or tolerant without a drink. It is the entire ritual that binds the group, not just the alcohol. And yet, in societies where alcohol is a routine, mundane, everyday, unexciting part of life, adolescents do not generally use it as a form of rebellion or stolen pleasure. Fox is not suggesting that the solution is to give "toddlers booze and flame throwers", only that the Australian 'risk averse' culture should be examined.[151]

The only effective message that might control negative or extremely anti-social or violent drinking behaviour is: "You are in control of your behaviour at all times. Drunkenness is no excuse."[152] St Vincent's should stick to this message, setting norms, which after all are one of the key goals of religious organisations, and leave taxation to the taxpayer and their governments.

---

[150] Fox 2015, 53.
[151] Fox 2015, 35.
[152] Fox 2015, 96.

8

Arrogant strategies crowd out effective alternatives

We cannot sit at the negotiating table with the people who caused this global disaster because one thing is crystal clear - this industry lies.[153]

-- Dr Vera Luiza da Costa e Silva, Head of the WHO FCTC Secretariat

Okay, Dr Silva, attacks on big tobacco are understandable, but the attacks, and the infantile behaviour on the part of the World Health Organization Framework Convention on Tobacco Control (Convention), undermine the efforts to assist the one billion smokers that WHO claim will remain at risk of ill health.[154] Further, "it is widely accepted that most smokers smoke for the nicotine but die from the other smoke constituents."[155] Delivering nicotine without the tobacco would seem a good option. But, WHO does not want to give Big Tobacco, which promotes some alternative products, a victory. It does not want to be seen to endorsing a product that may cause some harm. It prefers to remain pure.

Indeed, Public Health England, an agency of the Department of Health, found that "best estimates show e-cigarettes are 95 per cent

[153] Vera Luiza da Costa e Silva, Head of the World Health Organization Framework Convention on Tobacco Control Secretariat. Transparency, yes. interference, no. *The Huffington Post* 5 October 2016.

[154] V Bilano et al, 2015. Global trends and projections for tobacco use, 1990-2025. *The Lancet* 385 (9972), 966.

[155] Public Health England 2015, 14.

less harmful to your health than normal cigarettes."[156] Cancer Research UK-funded scientists found that people who swapped smoking regular cigarettes for e-cigarettes or nicotine replacement therapy for at least six months, had much lower levels of toxic and cancer causing substances in their body than people who continued to use conventional cigarettes.[157] And yet the Convention Parties (national signatories) will not entertain an open discussion of harm reduction which, given there are trials afoot to test their safety, would seem sensible.[158] It is understandable that public health advocates would not want to promote a harmful product, but to argue that "Even if e-cigarettes are significantly less harmful than conventional cigarettes, the product may have a very negative impact on public health if its use is spread to a large part of the population" says more about the value of the advocate than the science of public health.[159]

Rather than air these issues, the UN Framework Convention on Tobacco Control is a closed shop.[160] On its second day, the 2016 Convention (COP 7) voted to exclude the media and the public from observing proceedings, including being blocked from official tweets![161] The Australian delegates, sent by taxpayers, and representing a liberal democracy, did not stand up against this ban on free observation of debate conducted in the taxpayers' name, with taxpayers' money. They, and the Minister they represented, along with all other delegates, were a disgrace.

[156] Public Health England 2015, 5.
[157] L Shahab et al, 2017. Nicotine, carcinogen, and toxin exposure in long-term e-cigarette and nicotine replacement therapy users: a cross-sectional study. *Annals of Internal Medicine*, 7 February.
[158] Bullen et al 2013, 210.
[159] Pisinger 2014, 226.
[160] See Gary Johns, 2016. *Throw Open the Doors: the World Health Organization Framework Convention on Tobacco Control.* Brisbane: Connor Court.
[161] Drew Johnson, Reporters Banned From Global Anti-Tobacco Conference. *Daily Caller* 7 November 2016 and https://pbs.twimg.com/media/CwtzY4AVEAAeB-_.jpg:large

Why stifle debate?

Among recommendations to parties at its recent biennial meeting (COP 7) was "prevention of unproven health claims" being made about e-cigarettes. In most prejudicial language, it states, "Parties that have not banned the importation, sale, and distribution of [e-cigarettes] may consider prohibiting implicit or explicit claims about the effectiveness of [e-cigarettes] as smoking cessation aids unless a specialized governmental agency has approved them."[162] No mention of the Public Health England recommendation. The Convention shuns advice that it does not want to hear. As a consequence, the Secretariat does not have the expertise to deal with the challenges of finding a path for reduced harm alternatives to smoking.

The United Nations has learned the lessons of lack of legitimacy that stems from opaque decision-making. It has steadily embraced openness. The Convention, its Parties and Secretariat have not learned the lessons. Their restrictive behaviour is not the norm for UN debate. The UN welcomed world leaders, the media, external stakeholders and the public to the Paris Climate Change Conference in November 2015. Unlike Paris, the UN under the auspices of the WHO, convened an international gathering for COP 7, at which the public, media, industry, law enforcement and other key external stakeholders were barred from entry to numerous sessions.

At COP 5, Parties raised concerns over the numbers of tobacco industry representatives among public attendees. As a result, a decision was made to exclude members of the public at some meetings. At COP 6, essentially two proposals to control attendance were canvassed, each of them Orwellian. First, the public would be required to sign a written declaration affirming that they were not affiliated with the tobacco industry; if they were affiliated then they would not be issued

---

[162] WHO FCTC, Seventh Session Delhi, 2016. Electronic Nicotine Delivery Systems and Electronic Non-Nicotine Delivery Systems. *Provisional Agenda Item* 5.5.2, 7.

a badge.[163]

The second proposal was to create a new type of meeting during COPs, called "open meetings". Members of the public would be excluded but favoured observers allowed.[164] In fine diplomatic style, the two proposals were referred to a committee that recommended "consideration to providing options for maximizing transparency with regard to Party delegations, to COP and subsidiary bodies."[165]

The registration requirements for COP 7 were heavily scrutinised for any connection between the industry and observers and member delegates. Members of the public who wished to observe these publicly funded proceedings were forced to declare their affiliation. Anyone, including party delegates, that is, those who represent nations who pay for the Convention, was excluded if they had contact with the tobacco industry. It was reported that the COP 7 organisers wanted to exclude representatives from "state-owned tobacco industries" and "certain appointed and elected officials from executive, legislative and judicial branches."[166] This is difficult for those countries that have state-controlled tobacco companies, or officials who need to deal with tobacco companies on taxation and illicit trade in tobacco, or media representatives who have to report on the industry, or the common taxpayer or, heaven forbid, smokers.

The Convention will not permit any discussion or presentation on any matter by tobacco farmers, tobacco companies, retailers, or anybody who may raise divergent views of harm reduction and efforts to develop new products. For example, The Federation of All India Farmer Association had urged the Indian government to

---

[163] WHO FCTC, Sixth Session Moscow, 2014. Attendance of members of the public in meetings of the Conference of the Parties to the WHO FCTC and its subsidiary bodies. *Provisional Agenda Item 6.7*, 6.

[164] WHO FCTC, Sixth Session Moscow, 2014. *Verbatim Records Of Plenary Meetings*, 22.

[165] WHO FCTC, Sixth Session Moscow 2014, 80.

[166] Yael Ossowski, UN anti-tobacco meeting seeks to ban high-ranking government officials. *Huffington Post* 11 August 2016.

have representation of tobacco farmers at the COP 7.[167] Paris allowed organisations representing a diverse range of ideological perspectives (from ardent climate change activists to climate sceptics) to attend the meeting. The Convention barred all outside participation save for a select group of anti-tobacco organisations that were fully supportive of its agenda.

The United Nations engagement with stakeholders and civil society can never be a substitute for national constituencies and elected officials who provide democratic accountability. It must, therefore, always be open to scrutiny.[168] To be both removed from national constituencies and be a closed shop is fatal to good public policy. As Clive Bates, former Director of ASH United Kingdom, an anti-smoking NGO, has stated, "One wonders about the integrity of a process that is so fragile that it cannot tolerate dissenting voices."[169] Openness and effectiveness should be the Convention measure of success, not the intensity of dislike for opponents.

Harm reduction should not be ignored

The Convention has to wonder that, after all of its work, smoking persists. The prevalence of tobacco smoking among nations and demographic groups appears to follow a well-trodden path of rise and decline as nations develop, tastes change and consumers are better informed of the risks associated with tobacco consumption.[170] Significant reductions in smoking rates have been achieved in the United Kingdom, Australia, Brazil, and other countries. However,

---

[167] Tobacco farmers seek participation in Global Tobacco control summit. http://www.newkerala.com/news/2016/fullnews-100542.html accessed 26 August 2016.

[168] Gary Johns, 2004. Relations with nongovernmental organizations: lessons for the UN. *Seton Hall Journal of Diplomacy and International Relations* Summer/Fall, 51-65.

[169] Clive Bates, WHO plans e-cigarette offensive. *The Counterfactual* 17 April 2014.

[170] A Lopez et al, 1994. A descriptive model of the cigarette epidemic in developed countries. *Tobacco Control* 3, 242-7.

growing consumption in China and developing countries has offset these.[171] The Parties need to assess the Convention strategy knowing that a very large number of people to continue to consume tobacco.

Under the Convention, tobacco control means "a range of supply, demand and harm reduction strategies that aim to improve the health of a population by eliminating or reducing their consumption of tobacco products."[172] However, as Dr Derek Yach has pointed out, "The importance of harm reduction as a critical part of future tobacco control was recognized and is thus included in Article 1 of the FCTC."[173]

To be clear, harm reduction is not elsewhere mentioned in the Convention, which suggests hostility to the strategy at the outset. At the outset there was an understandable zeal to eliminate tobacco consumption. But that goal was always flawed. Despite advice to the contrary,[174] the WHO has pursued a single strategy of supply and demand reduction. It seems to have shunned a second strategy, which is to reduce the harm of smoking.[175] Undoubtedly, "deep distrust by many in the tobacco control movement" has driven a "reluctance to acknowledge the differential health risks [that] smokeless tobacco products could play in a harm reduction strategy."[176] But embracing

---

[171] *The Tobacco Atlas,* http://www.tobaccoatlas.org/topic/cigarette-use-globally/ accessed 15 July 2016.

[172] World Health Organization, 2005. *WHO Framework Convention on Tobacco Control,* 4.

[173] Derek Yach, Effective global tobacco control: time to engage health professionals, listen to smokers, and support harm reduction. *Vitality Global* 26 February 2016.

[174] K Stratton et al, 2001. Clearing the smoke: the science base for tobacco harm reduction. *Tobacco Control* 10(2), 189-95. M Zeller and D Hatsukami, 2009. The strategic dialogue on tobacco harm reduction: a vision and blueprint for action in the US. *Tobacco Control* 18(4) 324-32. D J Nutt et al, 2014. Estimating the harms of nicotine-containing products using the MCDA approach. *European Addiction Research* 20(2), 218-225.

[175] WHO urged the Parties at COP 6 2014, "to consider banning or restricting advertising, promotion and sponsorship of electronic nicotine delivery systems."

[176] A McNeill, et al, 2012. Whither tobacco product regulation? *Tobacco Control* 21(2), 225.

debate on differential risks among tobacco and nicotine products is likely to be a more promising strategy than hoping that all smokers will heed the call of the Convention and quit.

Under any realistic policy settings, it is entirely likely that tobacco smoking will remain a feature of human consumption, especially in some cultures, for example, China and Eastern and Southern Europe, and among certain parts of all societies, for example, lower socioeconomic groups.[177]

A strategy that ignores harm reduction in the hope of eliminating smoking is grievously flawed. Moreover, it appears that the 'elimination' strategy is itself running into trouble because, as one researcher has observed, "there is little relationship between tobacco control ... and prevalence."[178] If the elimination strategy is in doubt, and harm prevention strategies have been avoided, it is vital that governments are encouraged to think about opening debate on the lowest cost-most likely route to least harm.[179]

The Convention Secretariat is not taking the harm prevention route because it seems inured to the reality that the industry remains profitable and is unlikely to disappear even under the most stringent control regime.[180] The Secretariat seems oblivious to the fact that developed nations had already commenced tobacco reduction programs before the Convention was voted in, and developing nations are struggling to implement its provisions and rely on funds from developed nations, either taxpayers or philanthropists.[181] The Convention and its Secretariat are fighting the last war. The Convention has to ask itself: what is it doing for one billion smokers?

---

[177] *The Tobacco Atlas*, http://www.tobaccoatlas.org/topic/cigarette-use-globally/ accessed 15 July 2016.

[178] Clive Bates, Are you being manipulated? The wisdom of the WHO examined. *The Counterfactual* 2 June 2013.

[179] Clive Bates, WHO plans e-cigarette offensive. *The Counterfactual* 17 April 2014.

[180] MSCI, 2016, *World Tobacco Index*.

[181] Institute for Health Metrics and Evaluation, *Financing Global Health 2013*, 39.

Article 5.3 stifles debate

The underlying principle of Article 5.3 of the Convention, which is to ensure that the industry does not unduly influence tobacco control policies, is understandable. But the Secretariat goes as far as to consider that even open discussions and exchange of views, which represents a cornerstone of good policy-making, is problematic. As a result, the Secretariat uses Article 5.3 as an instrument to halt discussions altogether, including discussions of a wider risk strategy that could include harm reduction and realistic resourcing of anti-illicit trade strategies.

Instead of an open agenda, the Secretariat has pursued tactics which exclude technically proficient advisors, legitimate voices in the industry, and avoids public scrutiny. Article 5.3 of the Convention is a strong illustration of, and possible cause for, the failure of the Secretariat and the Parties to come to grips with the consumer marketplace, the unintended consequences of a reduction of supply, such as illicit trade, and the inadequate consideration given to the harm prevention side of the Convention.

Article 5.3 states that "Parties shall act to protect [tobacco control] policies from commercial and other vested interests of the tobacco industry in accordance with national law."[182] The guidelines, published by the Secretariat to elaborate Article 5.3, are highly inflammatory.

> The tobacco industry has operated for years with the express intention of subverting the role of governments and of WHO in implementing public health policies to combat the tobacco epidemic.
>
> Parties need to be alert to any efforts by the tobacco industry to undermine or subvert tobacco control efforts and the need

---

[182] WHO FCTC 2005, 7.

to be informed of activities of the tobacco industry that have a negative impact on tobacco control efforts.[183]

The Secretariat and the Parties seem unable to appreciate that the 'industry' consists of consumers, taxpayers, regulators, and tobacco corporations, all operating in a legal framework. The Secretariat appears to speak only to those whom it regards as its allies in a crusade to eliminate a harmful, yet legal, product. For example, Bhutan is held out as an example of total 'control' because it has banned the sale of tobacco products. But even here, tobacco may be imported for personal consumption, and while only 3.5 per cent of people in Bhutan smoke, 43 per cent consume smokeless tobacco in the form of Betal quid and chewing tobacco.[184] A study of the effect of the ban concluded that smoking remained a health problem for smokers and "that illegal tobacco smuggling including black market sales due to the sales ban in Bhutan remains robust.[185]

It is to be hoped that reports of a ban on tobacco in the 'highly authoritarian' Turkmenistan,[186] and a WHO FCTC meeting that took place there in April 2016, do not suggest that the Convention has veered down an authoritarian path in order to reach its goals of tobacco control.[187] Indeed, the WHO Europe office received the Bitaraplyk Order of Turkmenistan in recognition of their "collaboration with Turkmenistan over the past two decades on public health issues."[188]

---

[183] WHO FCTC, 2008. *Guidelines for Implementation of Article 5.3*, 1.

[184] Tobacco Control Laws, http://www.tobaccocontrollaws.org/legislation/country/bhutan/summary accessed 15 July 2016.

[185] Michael Givel, 2011. History of Bhutan's prohibition of cigarettes: Implications for neo-prohibitionists and their critics. *Drug Policy* 22(4), 306.

[186] Central Intelligence Agency, 2016. *The World Fact Book*.

[187] Matt Broomfield, Turkmenistan president outlaws all sales of tobacco products, effectively banning smoking altogether. *Independent* 17 January 2015.

[188] WHO Regional Office for Europe, WHO receives Turkmenistan State award for collaboration in public health. 21 July 2015.

Much of the Secretariat's energy is focussed on Article 5.3., which the Secretariat uses as an instrument to halt discussion of a wider risk strategy that should include harm reduction and realistic resourcing of anti-illicit trade strategies. The Secretariat and various NGOs have taken numerous actions in many forums to shut down debate.[189] In each case, courts of law or government officials have confirmed that Article 5.3 does not have the effect of banning contact between the tobacco industry and government. Nevertheless, although unsuccessful as a legal instrument against government, Article 5.3 has been used to empower public health advocates to promote preferred strategies. The use and abuse of Article 5.3 has had the effect of passing power from decision-makers in government to a group who cannot do the job because they are remote from responsible state regulators and in conflict with experienced international agencies.

Bureaucratic responses set in

A great deal of the Secretariat's effort is focussed on gathering Parties' reports. The Secretariat is mandated to consider the implementation reports that Parties are obliged to submit and to produce an annual summary of reports. These reports convey little about what is happening in individual nations and the conclusions that can be drawn from them about the successes and challenges of implementation are very general.[190] For example, although reporting 'steady progress', as of 2014, 27 per cent of Parties submitted no report whatsoever. The average implementation rate of the 'substantive' articles of the Convention 'approached' 60 per cent, which means that more than 40 per cent had not implemented

---

[189] See Johns 2016, 37-43.

[190] John Liberman, 2012. Four COPS and counting: achievements, under-achievements and looming challenges in the early life of the WHO FCTC Conference of the Parties. *Tobacco Control* 21(2), 218.

the substantive provisions.[191] Specifics are a different story again. Compliance with supply chain control 'tracking and tracing' is only 26 per cent, while 'collection of data on cross-border trade' is 53 per cent. Only 71 per cent of Parties have enacted legislation against illicit trade.[192]

This procedure appears to have deteriorated to a tick-the-box exercise on agreed measures of control in each nation. For example, the relationship between reporting control activities and prevalence reduction and, even more important, harm reduction, is very weak. The following observations from Clive Bates are in conjunction with the European ban on SNUS, used in Sweden as an alternative to tobacco smoking. Sweden scores well on smoking prevalence and low on cancers associated with tobacco, a much better record than UK and Ireland, but scores poorly on 'control activity', the compliance exercise the Convention encourages.

The UK and Ireland score highly on an index of tobacco control activity called the 'Tobacco Control Scale'.[193] The Index consists of scores and weightings for tobacco control measures, such as tax and price increases; bans on smoking in public places; consumer awareness campaigns; bans on advertising and promotion; prominence of health warnings; smoking cessation treatment and access to medicinal nicotine. Access to low-risk recreational nicotine alternatives to smoking is not assessed or recognised as part of tobacco control, so harm reduction does not count.[194]

---

191 World Health Organization Framework Convention on Tobacco Control, 2014. *Global Progress Report on the Implementation of the WHO Framework Convention on Tobacco Control.*
192 WHO FCTC 2014, 45.
193 For Europe see, L Joossens and M Raw, 2010. *The Tobacco Control Scale 2010 in Europe.* Association of European Cancer Leagues.
194 Bates, 2013.

The WHO FCTC is charged with the responsibility of controlling tobacco. It has, however, placed all of its policy eggs in the elimination basket when elimination is impossible. Surely, a parallel consideration of less harmful substitutes for tobacco would save more lives? Public health advocates, even in cases of direct harm, allow politics to get in the way of policy.

9

Public health competes with a host of other problems

Rather than focusing on obesity at the individual level, ... changes in food policies will need to be provided to low-income populations.[195]

-- Trishnee Bhurosy and Rajesh Jeewon, Health Sciences, University of Mauritius

Okay, Dr Bhurosy and Dr Jeewon, so tackling obesity in developing countries should shun individual choice and embrace 'food policies', which sounds suspiciously like the 'Smart food policies' encountered in chapter two, which, of course, is a very large endeavour. Public health officials find themselves in a world of pain when they face multiple complex problems, especially in developing countries. For example, Bangladeshis are encouraged to stop burning cigarettes and dung, but not coal. And yet coal may be the one thing they need to burn to a point where they can stop burning cigarettes and dung. They may, in time, also need to burn calories, but first things first.

It seems bizarre, for example, that some children in the United States are suing government officials because, they assert, the government has "known for decades that carbon dioxide pollution has been causing catastrophic climate change and has failed to take

---

[195] Trishnee Bhurosy and Rajesh Jeewon, 2014. Overweight and obesity epidemic in developing countries: a problem with diet, physical activity, or socioeconomic status? *The Scientific World Journal* 2014, article 964236.

necessary action to curtail fossil fuel emissions."[196] If only it were so easy. Sue a government and all will be well. Meanwhile, children in less developed countries face a multitude of sources of harm, only one of which is the risk to their health from poor choices. Their governments, and their parents, have to make difficult choices about what to do to tackle the risks they face.

Priorities is the stuff of good government

Bangladeshi's face multiple threats, some of which require individual choice, while others require collective choice. Setting priorities is essential in making successful choices. Every choice requires resources, and there is only so much to go around. For example, middle class Bangladeshis, and one day, working and lower class Bangladeshis, may experience obesity.[197] However, almost 45 per cent of Bangladeshi men smoke (and almost no women),[198] but women are probably as likely as men to die from lung cancer, heart disease, or stroke because as many as 88 per cent of households in Bangladesh cook with solid fuels, predominantly fuel wood but also agricultural residues and dung, from which women and children are most affected.[199] Almost all households using solid fuels cook over an open fire or an open stove. Exposure to particulates from these cooking practices may account for 150,000 deaths in Bangladesh each year, equivalent to about 15 per cent of deaths from all causes.[200]

Setting priorities, knowing what to do first, or most, is very difficult because each cause seems important and each cause has

---

[196] United States District Court for the District of Oregon. 2016. *Kelsey Cascade Rose Juliana et al versus The United States of America.* 6:15-cv-1517-TC, 2.
[197] Bhurosy and Jeewon 2014, 1.
[198] World Health Organization Framework Convention on Tobacco Control, 2014. *Reporting Instrument of The WHO Framework Convention On Tobacco Control* (Bangladesh).
[199] Bjorn Larsen, 2016. Benefits and costs of household cooking options for air pollution control. *Copenhagen Consensus Center,* 26.
[200] Larsen 2016, 3.

its champions. The causes near to the concerns of the public health lobby may not be the most important, or at least not in the immediate future, or may more easily be solved later as other matters are addressed. For example, the Bangladeshi government contributes just US$1,160 per year to the World Health Organization for Tobacco Control.[201] This may be a reflection of its regard for the World Health Organization but, clearly, it gives little priority to international efforts to stop Bangladeshi's smoking. It is as likely to give little priority to domestic efforts, despite smoking being a considerable source of harm.

Figure 4: Bangladesh priorities: benefits for every Taka spent

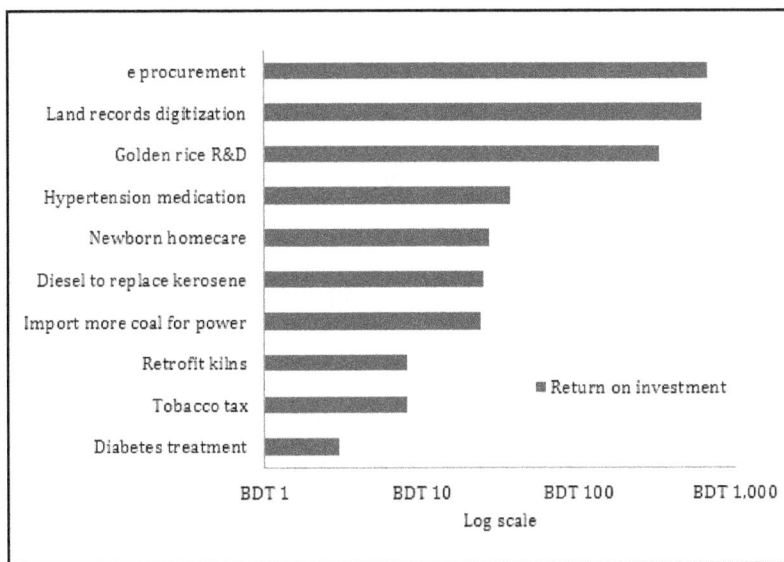

Source: Copenhagen Consensus Center, 2016. *Smarter Solutions for Bangladesh.* www.bangladesh-priorites.com

---

[201] World Health Organization Framework Convention On Tobacco Control Status of payments of voluntary assessed contributions as of 31 October 2016.

Work by Copenhagen Consensus economists, in conjunction with Bangladeshi scholars, has established priorities for Bangladesh on the basis of the best return on programs that would do the most good. Where do the classic public health prescriptions rank? On a range of social, economic and environmental issues, figure 4 sets out some of the priorities, ranked according to the best return for every Taka (BDT) spent. A tobacco tax and diabetes treatment come in at a very low return, well behind other contenders, even in direct health related areas such as hypertension medication (a cause of which may be related to tobacco) and newborn homecare. But other investments create much larger returns and these drive economic development which, all things being equal, improve health. It is worth considering four of these in detail.

Electronic government procurement

The outstanding investments for Bangladesh are investing in electronic procurement for government permits and contracts. This may seem trivial but the entire economy is tied up in paper and bureaucracy, so much so that every other venture is slowed. One Taka would generate a more than BDT600 return. Digitization of land records would generate similar returns; such is the drag on the economy, especially advancement in agricultural industries (which includes investment in research and development in golden rice) because of disputes over land title, and the difficulty of buying and selling land. The dampening effect on the Bangladeshi economy of these impediments is huge. Removing these restraints would create enormous wealth. Much health would follow.

Bangladeshi government procurement is fraught with inefficiency. Companies and contractors that want to provide goods and services to the government must currently apply for a tender in-person at a government office. Sometimes contractors who have political connections are best placed to win bids, or even to block other contractors who might be able to offer better prices. On other occasions, winning bidders subcontract the work to other firms, taking their own cut along the way and pushing costs higher.

These practices in public procurement can lead to delays, cost overruns, and output, which add up to higher costs for the government – which means higher cost to taxpayers. The effects of transforming the current procurement system into one that uses online systems show that electronic government procurement holds enormous potential benefits for the country – each taka spent on such efforts will do BDT663 of good.

The Local Government Engineering Department of Bangladesh is one of the four agencies that implemented 'e procurement'. Most of LGED procurement is for works, which also represent 73 per cent of all government procurement. Presently, about 95 per cent of LGED procurement uses e procurement. Before any project, LGED engineers make their own cost estimate for every item that will be procured. This provided a clear measure to track the effects of e procurement. Unsurprisingly, as more users adopted the practice, prices went down. The new price was typically 12 per cent lower.

The effects of expanding e procurement throughout the other 90 per cent of government procurement would be huge. The costs are straightforward. The majority goes toward purchasing computers and software. It will also require training staff to handle e procurement nation-wide as well as paying for operations and maintenance. The benefits would dwarf the costs.[202]

---

[202] Bjorn Lomborg, How e-GP save taxpayers tens of billions each year. *The Daily Star* 13 April 2016.

Retrofit kilns

The recommended and practical solution to death and harm by particulates is to encourage the use of improved biomass stoves or liquid petroleum gas stoves, that is, a fossil fuel. The estimate is to avoid 33,000 deaths.[203]

As many as 88 per cent of households in Bangladesh cook with solid fuels, predominantly fuelwood, but many also cook using agricultural residues and dung. The majority cook in a separate building while more than 20 per cent cook outdoors and 20 per cent cook in the house. Almost all households using solid fuels cook over open fire or an open stove. Nearly 150,000 people die in Bangladesh each year from particulate exposure, the equivalent to about 15 per cent of deaths from all causes. An assessment of benefits and costs of adopting cleaner cookstoves in Bangladesh evaluated three alternatives: improved biomass cookstoves; biomass gasifier stoves; and LPG stoves. Health improvements, biomass fuel savings, and cooking time savings benefits were assessed. Also assessed were stove purchase costs, stove maintenance, LPG fuel purchase, and costs of stove promotion programs.

An estimated 33,000 deaths may be avoided each year if all households were to adopt improved biomass cookstove and 91,000 of all households adopt gasifier stoves or LPG. Improved biomass cookstoves provide benefits that are up to seven times their cost. But health benefits of cooking with gasifier stoves or LPG are three times larger than cooking with an improved biomass cookstove. These stove solutions are, however, much more costly. Nevertheless, gasifier stoves provide benefit-cost ratios that are in the range of as much as seven, or nearly as high as for improved cookstoves. Benefit-cost ratios for LPG were much lower.[204] This program

---

[203]   Larsen 2016, 20.
[204]   Larsen 2016, 20.

would save more women and children than men.

While the two sources of harm, tobacco and particulates can be tackled at once, both require some government investment in information and regulation. In a world of competing priorities it is as well to be aware that a range of sources of harm exist and, that not all are of the same order as in developed countries. Retrofit kilns are not subject to personal choice. They are constrained by availability and cost. Hence, some government intervention may create significant change to cooking and consequent saved lives. Tobacco consumption may be less responsive because of personal choice.

Grow and adapt to climate

Bangladeshis do not have time to wait for children in the United States to sue their government for not taking sufficient action to avoid climate change. As fanciful as that proposition is, either that a suit could be successful or that the US government could do much about climate change, Bangladesh is vulnerable to rising sea levels. The mindset in Australia, the United States and Europe, is to stop digging and burning coal to lower the emissions from coal. The Bangladesh priority, however, is that it needs not less coal, but more. The benefits are more than 24 times the cost of increasing energy supply by importing coal even when accounting for the cost of increased greenhouse gas emissions.[205]

The question posed by researchers was: assuming that climate hazards increase with time, what was the best strategy for a poorly developed country like Bangladesh? The answer was that building resilience to climate change should be a top priority of a development strategy. Structural changes of the Bangladeshi economy, with a

---

[205] Herath Gunatilake and David Roland-Holst, 2016. Smart Energy options for Bangladesh: Bangladesh priorities. *Copenhagen Consensus Center*, 43.

correspondingly significant increase in productivity of agriculture, manufacturing, services and so on, was the only way to become a middle-income country.[206]

Relatively low Gross Domestic Product creates an obvious constraint to mobilise resources for adaptation. Various development priorities are in competition for public money and multilateral development assistance. Society may invest in carbon intensive energy, buy very productive technologies and accumulate enough resources to tackle climate change successfully. Or, it could spend its money trying to abate carbon dioxide emissions.

These same questions are relevant to developed countries but, they at least have the flexibility to choose to abate, as ineffective a response as it is. The question for Bangladesh is how much it should spend on abatement and how much on adaptation. Should it build cyclone shelters or shift the population to higher grounds? Should it build higher barriers to withstand rising waters or build a stronger economy to pay for them?

The research provided definite answers. Relocation of population inland was the most efficient risk mitigation intervention. The researchers recommended that during the next 20 years around one million people currently exposed to a high cyclone threat (and these occur regardless of climate change) should be relocated. The most promising intervention would be relocation of population into second-tier cities with simultaneous training and investment in education.[207] Polders reconstruction and reinforcement requires a selective approach. Also, large investments should be delayed until major uncertainty on intensity of future climate change is resolved or significantly narrowed. Relocation could be scaled up in response to more severe climate conditions or in response to higher increase

---

[206] Alexander Golub and Elena Strukova Golub, 2016. Cost-benefit analysis of adaptation strategy in Bangladesh. *Copenhagen Consensus Center*, 14.
[207] Golub and Golub 2016, 52.

of productivity in agriculture and in the manufacturing sector.[208] Adoption of a structural transformation strategy of employment in Bangladesh in favour of the manufacturing sector is a fundamental precondition to build resilience to climate change.

Further, increased productivity is critical for economic development. Agriculture has a significant room for improvement and this intervention yields a high return. Most of the benefits in agriculture are realisable, but there are significant barriers to adoption of new more productive technologies. Institutional changes to promote deployment of new technologies are crucial for climate change resilience. Mangroves protection is also an important interim intervention. It yields the third highest returns. This intervention is important in the mid-term as it helps by buying time for gradual reallocation.

Bangladeshis need coal

And what would help drive this combination of climate change responses? Cheap energy: gas and coal. The researchers concluded that diversifying the fuel mix in the power sector was a critical need for long-term energy security in Bangladesh. In particular, coal would be a cost effective fuel for Bangladesh's electric power sector.[209] Domestically produced natural gas provides a majority of Bangladesh's commercial energy. The country has limited alternatives and will continue to rely primarily on this energy source to fuel its development.

Bangladesh imports to meet most of its oil needs, and remains very dependent on biomass for domestic energy production, particularly in rural areas. Despite once abundant resource endowments, the

---

[208] Golub and Golub 2016, 58.
[209] Gunatilake and Roland-Holst 2016, 14.

country suffers from endemic energy poverty, and 96 million people remain without access to electricity. The country's electrification rate of 50 per cent is far below that of its neighbours India (75 per cent), and Sri Lanka (95 per cent). Lack of access to electricity remains one of the country's main development challenges.

Per capita electric power consumption in Bangladesh is among the world's lowest, even after taking account of relatively high poverty incidence. This suggests that the country's economy grows despite serious energy constraints, yet current trends suggest that even this resilience is at risk. Almost three-quarters of Bangladesh's population live in rural areas, and about half are employed in agriculture, and the national electric power sector is more appropriate to that of an agrarian society. If the economy aspires to more energy-intensive industrialisation and urbanisation like developed countries, electrification and energy production will have to expand substantially.

The research strongly suggested that gas can generate better economic values in household cooking, transport, and industry sectors. It also confirms the higher value addition of gas in these sectors. Using coal for electricity generation would free the government from subsidies to the gas sector without facing energy cost escalation. Making coal a primary electric power fuel would reduce domestic energy costs and allow the economy to experience higher real consumption, savings, and investment among households and enterprises. Switching to more cost-effective electric power while reforming gas prices to respond to market forces would take real Bangladeshi GDP 4.5 per cent higher by 2030. The growth increment would be about 25 per cent under combined impacts of gas price increase, energy efficiency improvement, fertilizer subsidy, together with diversification of the fuel mix in power sector.

Fuel source diversification with coal is not without additional costs. The carbon emissions increase by about 20 per cent from the baseline. It may also be observed that, despite its negative environmental reputation, electric power would be a good place to introduce coal, as its emissions would be more concentrated and thereby easier to monitor and manage.

In distributed use, for example, transport, household heating, and cooking, gas would be more appropriate for converse reasons. The coal scenario results highlight one of the major development challenges facing developing countries, the use of low cost fuel to enhance development results in more carbon emissions. This problem can be ameliorated to some extent by using clean coal technologies such as super critical and ultra super critical coal technologies.

Into this mix of priorities for Bangladeshis are public health standards: hypertension interventions and newborn homecare for babies and mothers. Classic public health concerns and prescriptions, tobacco tax and diabetes treatment, rank very lowly among other priorities. Most intriguing, Bangladeshis need to have access to clean domestic cookers for better health, and burn coal and gas to lift their country out of poverty, the better to respond to all sources of harm, including tobacco and obesity.

It is highly unlikely that a strong public health lobby would have reached these conclusions. The mindset would be to tell Bangladeshi's what is good for them rather than let Bangladeshis pursue the satisfaction of their needs, in time better to respond to any source of harm. The public health lobby, which the literature suggests includes an abatement rather than adaptation mindset, would have created a great deal of waste and harm had they been the dominant source of public policy.

10

What to do about the public health lobby

*As doctors, the government's performance [on climate change] is
inadequate.* [210]
-- Dr David Shearman, Doctors for the Environment
Australia

Okay, Dr Shearman, what is it that doctors, as a consequence of their
training, know about climate change? Without canvassing the climate
change debate, it is possible that there is little that governments can
do to forestall changes to the earth's atmosphere, and associated
weather, but in trying to do so they could do harm.

Medical doctors are not at all well placed to assess risk in
public policy. Indeed, they may be the least qualified as, except in
emergencies, they are invested in helping any and all. Doctors may
have skills in medical triage, the ability to set priorities on the basis
of short-term medical risk, but as we have seen in the Bangladeshi
example, policy triage is another world. The David Shearmans of
the world are well meaning, but their medical qualifications are as
likely to mislead as lead on policy. They are, naturally, more than
welcome as citizens to try their hand, but that is not how they
market themselves.

It is not as if governments have not been legislating matters
of harm for many years. These may affect consumers directly, but
it is more likely governments operate on corporations as entities

---

[210] David Shearman, Emeritus Professor of Medicine at the University of Adelaide and
the Secretary of Doctors for the Environment. Doctors prescribe open mind on
climate policy. *ABC News Radio* 8 December 2016.

'responsible' for harm. There is, as a consequence, a massive array of state regulation imposed on corporations. Typically, national regulators such as the Australian Competition and Consumer Commission 'promote competition', 'remedy market failure', and 'protect the interests and safety of consumers'. In addition, other regulation secures fair dealings with contractors and creditors, protection for workers and compliance with environmental standards. As a result, among much other legislation, the *Corporations Act 2001* (Cth) in Australia contains more than 3000 pages, and there are more than 1600 pages of corporate regulations made under the Act.[211]

Where public health advocates cannot succeed in having parliaments impose even greater restrictions on corporations, they seek to bypass democratic regulation by de-normalising corporations. In effect, they seek to superimpose civil regulation. If only Coca-Cola would stop making Coca-Cola all would be well.[212] If only McDonald's would stop making hamburgers,[213] or bet 365 stop making gambling readily available, or Diageo stop making Johnny Walker or Guinness. Instead, advocates have reversed the onus and sought to portray some corporations as inherently harmful. Advocates use concepts such as 'corporate social responsibility' and 'social license to operate' to have corporations prove their worth as a sort of civil regulation. Civil regulation may lack the legal authority and power of government regulation, but it works sufficiently to convince some corporates of their 'original sins'.

This technique is nowhere more prominent than in demonisation of personal habits and consumption. Building on success in the

---

[211] The Parliament of the Commonwealth of Australia, *Corporations Act 2001* (Cth).
[212] The NGO Praxis Project is seeking to stop Coca-Cola and the American Beverage Association from deceptive advertising of sugary drinks, particularly to children, and for the disclosure of documents related to their impact on health. U.S. District Court, Northern District of California (Oakland) *The Praxis Project v. The Coca-Cola Co.*, 17-cv-00016.
[213] In 2014, local residents in Tecoma, Victoria tried to stop McDonalds from opening a shop in the town. http://www.burgeroff.org accessed 6 January 2016.

control of tobacco products, 'public health' advocates are now on the warpath against gambling, alcohol, sugar and much more. Despite a hefty burden of national and international regulation and success in informing consumers and mitigating the harm of legal products (visit the websites of any of the above manufacturers), advocates have moved beyond regulation, going to extraordinary lengths to de-normalise corporations in these fields.

Disinvestment: an expensive indulgence

A popular political tactic among health and allied advocates is to call for disinvestment, among superannuation and other investment funds, in 'sin' industries. The suggestion is usually accompanied by gushing 'boosterism' for returns from 'ethical' investment at equal or higher returns. Alas, the truth is that sin industries are generally more profitable than 'ethical' ones. Doing the right thing, therefore, will harm investors. A stark example is two United States mutual funds launched in the early 2000s.

Figure 5. Vice Fund versus Vanguard Fund

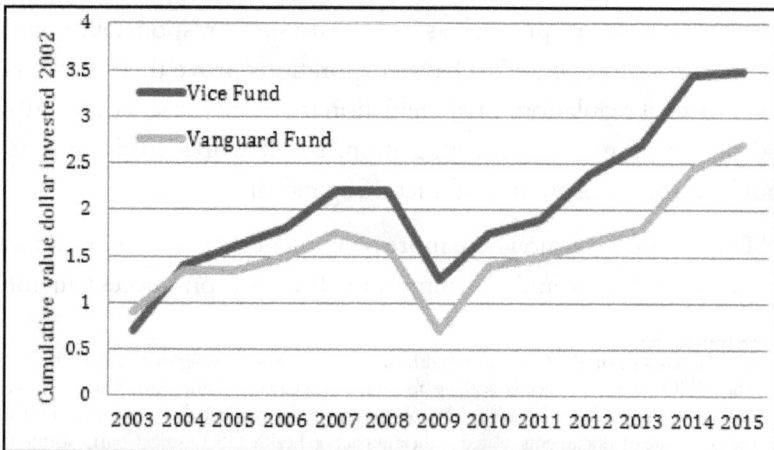

Source: Adapted from Elroy Dimson, Paul Marsh and Mike Staunton, 2015. Responsible investing: does it pay to be bad? *Credit Suisse Research Institute, 18.*

The Vice Fund invests in businesses that are considered by many to be socially irresponsible. Recently renamed the Barrier Fund, it has assets of USD $290 million invested in tobacco, alcoholic beverage, gaming and defense/aerospace industries. By contrast, the Vanguard Fund (FTSE Social Index) tracks an index screened by social, human rights, and environmental criteria. Constituents have allegedly superior environmental policies, strong hiring/promotion records for ethnic or religious minorities and women, and a safe workplace. There are no companies involved in tobacco, alcohol, adult entertainment, firearms, gambling, nuclear power, and unfair labour practices.

Figure 5 illustrates the cumulative returns from the two funds. The relative winner was the Vice Fund, whose investment performance earned it a top rating from various rating agencies. The Vanguard Fund, which had lower investment growth during the same interval, was the relative loser. Many ethical investors consider that investing in 'responsible and principled' companies is likely to be rewarded in the long run by better stock market performance. Unfortunately, for them and their clients, the evidence suggests that 'sin' pays. Investments in 'unethical' stocks, industries and countries have tended to outperform the 'ethical'.

Ironically, responsible investors should recognise that they may be partly responsible for the higher returns from sin. The argument is that irresponsible businesses can be disciplined by the threat of divestment of the firm's shares. The assumption is that downward pressure on the share price will make the company less valuable, pushing up its cost of capital to the detriment of its ability to raise finance, and possibly raising the likelihood of a takeover bid.

It can be profitable, however, to invest in stocks that ethical investors abhor. The rationale for 'vice investing' is that these companies have a steady demand for their goods and services regardless of economic conditions. They operate globally, they tend to be high-margin businesses, and they are in industries with high entry barriers. Yet, if a large enough proportion of investors avoids 'vice' businesses, their share prices will be depressed relative to fundamentals. If companies have a lower stock price, they offer a buying opportunity to investors who are untroubled by ethical considerations.[214] For example, they may trade at a lower price-earnings or lower price-dividend ratio. Buying them would then offer a superior expected financial return, which, for some investors, compensates for the emotional 'cost' of exposure to offensive companies.[215]

Is health promotion or harm prevention charitable?

Many public health advocates operate through NGOs, some of which have charity status. This status proves a further, and final, ground for criticism of public health advocacy.

If charity incentives cost the taxpayer money via foregone revenue, 'the point of charity law had better be a good one'.[216] So argued a staunch supporter of the charity sector. Taxpayers should not subsidise politically contestable actions or subsidise free speech and yet, this is exactly what happens in the public health arena. Good policy is judged over long periods through democratic means. When governments support "one reasonable conception of 'the good' over any other", however, by subsidising charities that spruik controversial public policy it brings the sector down and it

---

[214] Dan Ahrens, 2007. *Investing in Vice: The Recession Proof Portfolio of Booze, Bets, Bombs and Butts.* St. Martin's Press (electronic).

[215] Elroy Dimson et al, 2015. Responsible investing: does it pay to be bad? *Credit Suisse Research Institute*, 20.

[216] M Harding, 2011. What is the point of charity law? *Curent Legal Issues Seminar.* Brisbane: Bar Association of Queensland, 2.

dishonours at least some taxpayers.[217] The many arguments outlined above should indicate to any government and any donor that even in the health arena, and with seeming straightforward wrongs to right, public health lobby policy prescriptions are often just plain wrong. Some charities, and indeed, some government health departments, undertake work that is too exposed to political aims. The arguments and evidence above suggests that health promotion falls into this category.

Health Promotion Charities and Harm Prevention Charitable Institutions in Australia are very strange beasts.[218] Every citizen has free access to hospital care and highly subsidised access to a general practitioner who can advise about their health, including all of the issues that HPCs and HPCIs 'promote'. These organisations are also eligible to receive endorsement as a Deductible Gift Recipient, which means that donors get a tax break from making donations to the organisation. It also means that taxpayers subsidise their advocacy.[219] Given the extent to which such advocacy is misplaced or misleading, this is a bad public policy. Why should the taxpayer subsidise further, less professional, advice than that which can be obtained from a general practitioner or, indeed, a medical specialist?

The rules governing charity advocacy are reasonably clear and, frankly, very generous. For an organisation to be a charity it must be established for charitable purposes that are for the public benefit. An organisation will not be charitable if it has disqualifying political purposes. Advocacy and campaigning can be a legitimate and effective way of furthering the charitable purposes of a charity. It is important, however, that charities do not cross the line into having a

---

[217] S W McCormack, 2010. Taking the good with the bad: recognizing the negative externalities created by charities and their implications for the charitable deduction. *Arizona Law Review* 52, 1025.

[218] See Australian Government Department of Social Security, Register of Harm Prevention Charities - Deductible Gift Register.

[219] Justice Connect Not-for-profit Law, 2014. *Guide to Deductible Gift Recipient Status*, 24.

disqualifying political purpose and that they maintain independence from party politics. This is pretty easy to maintain. A charity's policy position on a matter of concern may be similar to, or align with that of, a particular political party. In such a situation it is permissible for the charity to continue to campaign on that issue, provided that this does not amount to the charity having a purpose of promoting or opposing a particular political party or candidate.[220]

The report in 2016 of the House of Representatives Environment Committee into the Register of Environmental Organisations had something to say about advocacy as a charitable purpose. The committee recommended that legislative and administrative changes be pursued by the Australian Taxation Office (ATO) to require that the value of each environmental deductible gift recipient's annual expenditure on environmental remediation work be no less than 25 per cent of the organisation's annual expenditure from its public fund.[221] Such a rule, with equivalent health deeds, applied to public health charities would be a good thing.

Aid/Watch Incorporated v. Commissioner of Taxation

The move to free up the charity voice in political fields took a decisive step towards publicly subsidised free speech in a recent case in the High Court of Australia. As a consequence of a decision of the High Court in 2010 in *Aid/Watch Incorporated v. Commissioner of Taxation*, charities are arguably free to lobby government and do little, if any, charity work. When charities lobby government on

---

[220] Australian Charities and Not-for-Profits Commission, 2016. Political campaigning and advocacy by registered charities: what you need to know.

[221] The Parliament of the Commonwealth of Australia, 2016. *Inquiry into the Register of Environmental Organisations House of Representatives Standing Committee on the Environment.*

controversial matters, using the privilege of charity status, should the taxpayer have a right of veto?

Charities in Australia have always been free to lobby so long as they maintained charity work as their dominant purpose. The High Court decided that a charity engaged in "lawful means of public debate concerning the efficiency of foreign aid directed to the relief of poverty is a purpose beneficial to the community."[222] Justice Heydon, in the minority judgment, found that "Aid/Watch did not have the goal of relieving poverty. It provided no funds, goods or services to the poor."[223] Justice Kiefel, in the minority, decided that Aid/Watch's "pursuit of a freedom to communicate its views does not qualify as being for the public benefit."[224]

If the ATO had challenged a charity set up to cut foreign aid, arguably a public benefit, the High Court would have run a mile. The Australian Government has written the substance of the High Court decision into law to legitimise "promoting or opposing a change to any matter established by law, policy or practice in the Commonwealth, a state, a territory or another country."[225] Advocacy and lobbying have become charitable purposes. Charities will be less constrained to lobby and less constrained to do less charity.

How much lobbying charities can undertake, that is, how much charitable resource they devote to politics, is a moot point. Historically, a "trust for the attainment of political objects" was invalid because courts had "no means of judging whether a proposed change in the law would or would not be for the public benefit."[226] The High Court overlooked this matter in *Aid/Watch* and decided that an association

---

[222] *Aid/Watch Incorporated v Commissioner of Taxation* [2010] HCA 42 (1 December 2010), 47.

[223] *Aid/Watch*, 60.

[224] *Aid/Watch*, 86.

[225] The Parliament of the Commonwealth of Australia, *Charities Act 2013* (Cth), Part 3 Division 1(12).

[226] Halsbury's, 2013. *Laws of Australia*. LexisNexis Butterworths 75, 290.

engaged in researching, monitoring and campaigning on delivery of overseas aid should maintain charitable status.

The Court ruled that there is no general doctrine that excludes political objects from charitable purposes. Although the Court indicated that certain forms of advocacy would not be denied charitable status, it did not align the objects of political parties with charity, and so it remains a non-charitable object to promote education in and promulgation of the views of a political party. The High Court failed to notice, however, that *Aid/Watch* did no charity work whatsoever, and that there was no restriction on its free speech, only that it was subsidised by the public purse to pursue its political objectives.

The majority did not go so far as to say or decide that generating public debate about *any* or *every* government activity or policy, or the absence of a policy on a particular subject matter, would fall within a charitable purpose. Whether the generation of public debate about a particular government activity or policy that lies beyond existing heads of charity can be a charitable purpose will be a matter to be considered on a case-by-case basis. The majority in the High Court, in finding in favour of *Aid/Watch* on the basis that it was a body having purposes beneficial to the community, did not deal with the correctness or otherwise of the Full Federal Court's findings which the High Court overturned.[227]

Charities lobby government because they reckon it pays dividends. The results of a recent United States study of not-for-profits (charities) indicate that a 10 per cent increase in lobbying expenditures produces a 0.5 per cent increase in contributions.[228] But contributions are not the only gains from lobbying; it can bring

---

[227] Australian Taxation Office, Legal Data Base, *Decision Impact Statement, Aid/Watch*.

[228] Jill Nicholson-Crotty, 2011. Does reported policy activity reduce contributions to nonprofit service providers? *Policy Studies Journal* 39(4), 599.

money and favourable rule changes to the cause. That does not hold necessarily for every other cause. Lobbying, just as every other activity, has opportunity cost. It requires resources that otherwise could have been put to productive use. It may have a negative impact on economic activity. A recent study suggests, "the higher the quality of economic institutions, the more costly is lobbying with respect to growth." It depends on "whether pressure enhances or inhibits institutions that foster economic freedom."[229]

Maybe NGOs need social licence as much as any business

Public health charities make all of the same mistakes as every other lobby. Why the taxpayer would favour them is a mystery. If public health charities want to be civil regulators, the presumption of righteousness needs to be tested. Perhaps they, too, should have a social license to operate.[230] At the very least, taxpayers should never subsidise campaigning charities. The *AID/Watch* decision and the amendments to the *Charities Act* to allow an unspecified amount of lobbying should be scrapped. A standard pro-NGO academic view is that governments view charities and other NGOs as necessary actors that provide access to information, serve as a vehicle for aggregating preferences, and help coordinate the political process, rather than as threats to the status quo. They might argue that governments are likely to remove barriers and facilitate access to resources to encourage NGO formation.[231]

With nary a thought, academics seem unable to recognise that

---

[229] J C Heckelman and B Wilson, 2013. Institutions, lobbying, and economic performance. *Economics and Politics* 25(3), 360.

[230] John Morrison, 2014. *Social Licence: How To Keep Your Organisation Legitimate*. London: Palgrave McMillan.

[231] Elizabeth Bloodgood et al, 2013. National styles of NGO regulation. *Nonprofit and Voluntary Sector Quarterly* 43(4), 719.

governments encourage NGOs to lobby government, to reinforce the enduring relevance of government to the voter. There is no guarantee of better policy in publicly subsidised public health lobbying. It might be argued, from a pluralist perspective, that charities and NGOs provide valuable services by giving a voice to segments of the population that would otherwise have difficulty finding representation in elite or for-profit institutions. Which is very sweet, but most of those in public health charities are the elite. They are privileged health workers, using their science to poor public policy ends.

Demanding a social license to operate for NGOs may be problematic, as a more sensible aim should be to minimise all regulation. Governments, however, should develop protocols for dealing with NGOs in which they should declare their dealings with NGOs and all funding which goes to NGOs. Do-gooders, even when they are doing good, often get it wrong. No group that espouses saving others from harm should receive any privilege from the taxpayer. Why should the taxpayer pay to have someone tell them how to live and then lobby government to tax them for the privilege?

The numerous public health NGOs featured in this essay have similar motivations: to help prevent ill health among those who choose to consume products that may damage their health. But each NGO, or in some cases, government health departments with proselytising public health officials, find it difficult to account for the consumer satisfaction derived from the consumption of the allegedly harmful product. Nor is the product harmful in all cases, nor is it harmful in all amounts. Advocates often over-state their case and use their white coats to push nonsense evidence of harm and cost. They think that your body belongs to the nation.

References

Aid/Watch Incorporated v Commissioner of Taxation [2010] HCA 42 (1 December 2010).

J J Anderson, 2016. Adiposity among 132479 UK Biobank participants; contribution of sugar intake vs other macronutrients. *International Journal of Epidemiology* July 2016.

ACIL Allen, 2014. *Counting the Costs of Alcohol Policy-relevant Costs to Australia.*

Dan Ahrens, 2007. *Investing in Vice: The Recession Proof Portfolio of Booze, Bets, Bombs and Butts.* St. Martin's Press (electronic).

Olivier Allais et al, 2010. The effects of a fat tax on French households' purchases: a nutritional approach. *American Journal of Agricultural Economics* 92(1).

Australian Bureau of Statistics, 2007. *Australian Social Trends, 2006.*

Australian Bureau of Statistics, 2010. *Year Book Australia, 2009-10.*

Australian Bureau of Statistics, 2014. *Australian Health Survey: Nutrition First Results: Foods and Nutrients, 2011-12.*

Australian Bureau of Statistics 2014. *Australian Historical Population Statistics, 2014.*

Australian Bureau of Statistics 2014. *Deaths, Australia, 2013*

Australian Bureau of Statistics, 2014. *Measures of Australia's Progress, 2013.*

Australian Bureau of Statistics, 2015. *Apparent Consumption of Alcohol, Australia* (series).

Australian Bureau of Statistics, 2015. *Apparent Consumption of Alcohol, Australia, 2013-14.*

Australian Bureau of Statistics, 2015. *Births, Australia 2014.*

Australian Bureau of Statistics, 2016. *Australian Health Survey: Consumption of Added Sugars 2011-12.*

Australian Charities and Not-for-profits Commission, 2015. Commissioner's interpretation statement: health promotion charities. *CIS 2015/01.*

Australian Institute of Health and Welfare, 2012. *Australia's Health 2012.*

Australian Institute of Health and Welfare, 2014. Healthy life expectancy in Australia: patterns and trends 1998 to 2012. *Bulletin 126.*

Australian Institute of Health and Welfare, 2016. *Impact and Causes of Illness and Deaths in Australia 2011.*

Australian Productivity Commission, 2010. *Gambling.*

Australian Safety and Compensation Council, 2006. *Estimating the Number of Work-related Traumatic Injury Fatalities in Australia 2003-2004.*

Australia's Future Tax System, 2009. *Final Report.*

van Baal et al, 2008. Lifetime medical costs of obesity: prevention no cure for increasing health expenditure. *PLOS Medicine,* 0242.

Gary Banks, 2011. Evidence and social policy: the case of gambling. *Presentation to South Australian Centre for Economic Studies, Corporate Seminar,* Adelaide, 30 March.

Trishnee Bhurosy and Rajesh Jeewon, 2014. Overweight and obesity epidemic in developing countries: a problem with diet, physical activity, or socioeconomic status? *The Scientific World Journal* 2014, article 964236.

V Bilano et al, 2015. Global trends and projections for tobacco use, 1990-2025. *The Lancet* 385 (9972).

Elizabeth Bloodgood et al, 2013. National styles of NGO regulation. *Nonprofit and Voluntary Sector Quarterly* 43(4).

Malene Bødker et al, 2015(a). The Danish fat tax: effects on consumption patterns and risk of ischaemic heart disease. *Preventive Medicine* 77.

Malene Bødker et al, 2015(b). The rise and fall of the world's first fat tax. *Health Policy* 119.

Thomas Buchmueller and Johar Meliyanni, 2015. Obesity and health expenditures: evidence from Australia. *Economics and Human Biology* 17.

C Bullen et al, 2013. Study protocol for a randomised controlled trial of electronic cigarettes versus nicotine patch for smoking cessation. *BMC Public Health* 13.

Linda Byrne et al, 2011. Parental status and childhood obesity in Australia. *International Journal of Pediatric Obesity* 6.

Joshua Byrnes et al, 2013. Can harms associated with high-intensity drinking be reduced by increasing the price of alcohol? *Drug and Alcohol Review* 32(1).

Campaign for Tobacco-Free Kids, 2008. A decade of broken promises: the 1998 state tobacco settlement ten years later. *Robert Wood Johnson Foundation*.

Margaret Chan. Address at the 133rd Inter-Parliamentary Union Assembly Geneva, Switzerland, 19 October 2015.

Deborah Cobb-Clark, 2010. Disadvantage across the generations. *Insights* 8.

Linda Cobiac et al, 2017. Taxes and subsidies for improving diet and population health in Australia: a cost- effectiveness modelling study. *PLOS ONE* 14(2).

Stephen Colagiuri, 2016. Is obesity a disease?: economic implications. *Obesity Australia Summit Papers*.

David Collins and Helen Lapsley, 2008. The costs of tobacco, alcohol and illicit drug abuse to Australian society in 2004-05. Department of Health and Ageing. *Monograph Series no. 64*.

Tracy Comans et al, 2013. The cost-effectiveness and consumer acceptability of taxation strategies to reduce rates of overweight and obesity among children in Australia: study protocol. *BMC Public Health* 13(1182).

Commission on Social Determinants of Health, 2008. *Closing the Gap in a Generation*. Geneva: World Health Organization.

Copenhagen Consensus Center, 2016. *Smarter Solutions for Bangladesh*.

Eric Crampton, 2008. Cost-benefit analysis when the conclusion drives the method: a review of 'report on tobacco taxation in New Zealand'. *The New Zealand Medical Journal* 121(1269).

Galina Daraganova and Lukar Thornton, 2013. Eating behaviour: socio-economic determinants and parental influence. *Longitudinal Study of Australian Children Annual Statistical Report 2013*.

Nicole Darmon et al, 2014. Food price policies improve diet quality while increasing socioeconomic inequalities in nutrition. *The International Journal of Behavioral Nutrition and Physical Activity* 11(1).

Data Analysis Australia Pty Ltd, 2014. How often does a night out lead to an assault. *Unpublished.*

Sinclair Davidson, 2016. *Submission to Parliamentary Joint Committee on Law Enforcement Inquiry into Illicit Tobacco*. Australian Parliament.

Liam Delaney et al, 2013. Why do some Irish drink so much? Family, historical and regional effects on students' alcohol consumption and subjective normative thresholds. *Review of Economics of the Household* 11(1).

Department of Health Victoria, Prevention and Population Health Branch, 2013. *Healthy Choices: Healthy Eating Policy and Catering Guide for Workplaces*.

Elroy Dimson et al, 2015. Responsible investing: does it pay to be bad? *Credit Suisse Research Institute*.

Paul Downward and Peter Dawson, 2016. Is it pleasure or health from leisure that we benefit from most? An analysis of well-being alternatives and implications for policy. *Social Indicators Research* 126(1).

Stephen Duckett and Hal Swerissen, 2016. *A Sugary Drinks Tax: Recovering the Community Costs of Obesity*. Melbourne: Grattan Institute.

Ryan Edwards, 2011. Commentary: soda taxes, obesity, and the shifty behavior of consumers. *Preventive Medicine* 52(6).

Jason Fletcher et al, 2010. Can soft drink taxes reduce population weight? *Contemporary Economic Policy* 28(1).

Jason Fletcher et al, 2010. The effects of soft drink taxes on child and adolescent consumption and weight outcomes. *Journal of Public Economics* 94.

Foundation for Alcohol Research and Education, 2012. *Annual Report 2011-12*.

Foundation for Alcohol Research and Education, 2015. *Annual Financial Report 2014-15*.

Anne Fox, 2015. Understanding behaviour in the Australian and New Zealand night-time economies: an anthropological study. *Unpublished.*

James Fries, 2005. The compression of morbidity. *The Milbank Quarterly* 83(4).

K. Fujioka, 2015. Current and emerging medications for overweight or obesity in people with comorbidities. *Diabetes, Obesity and Metabolism* 17.

Maxim Gakh, 2015. Law, the health in all policies approach, and cross-sector collaboration. *Public Health Reports* 130(1).

Michael Gannon, Health: the best investment that a nation can make. 17 August 2016 *National Press Club Address*, Canberra.

Michael Givel, 2011. History of Bhutan's prohibition of cigarettes: implications for neo-prohibitionists and their critics. *Drug Policy* 22(4).

Alexander Golub and Elena Strukova Golub, 2016. Cost-benefit analysis of adaptation strategy in Bangladesh. *Copenhagen Consensus Center.*

Herath Gunatilake and David Roland-Holst, 2016. Smart energy options for Bangladesh: Bangladesh priorities. *Copenhagen Consensus Center.*

Halsbury's, 2013. *Laws of Australia.* LexisNexis Butterworths.

Clive Hamilton and Sarah Maddison, 2007. *Silencing Dissent: How the Australian Government is Controlling Public Opinion and Stifling Debate.* Sydney: Allen & Unwin.

Andrew Hanks et al, 2013. From Coke to Coors: a field study of a fat tax and its unintended consequences. *Journal of Nutrition Education and Behaviour* 45(4), Supplement, July-August, S40.

Andrew Hanks et al, 2014. Chocolate milk consequences: a pilot study evaluating the consequences of banning chocolate milk in school cafeterias. *PLOS ONE* 9(4).

M Harding, 2011. What is the point of charity law? *Current Legal Issues Seminar.* Brisbane: Bar Association of Queensland.

Corinna Hawkes et al, 2015. Smart food policies for obesity prevention. *The Lancet* 385(9985).

J C Heckelman and B Wilson, 2013. Institutions, lobbying, and economic performance. *Economics and Politics* 25(3).

Gillie Hendrie et al, 2014. Greenhouse gas emissions and the Australian diet: comparing dietary recommendations with average intakes. *Nutrients* 6.

Institute for Health Metrics and Evaluation, *Financing Global Health 2013*.

Jørgen Dejgård Jensen and Sinne Smed, 2013. The Danish tax on saturated fat: short run effects on consumption, substitution patterns and consumer prices of fats. *Food Policy* 42.

Gary Johns, 2004. Relations with nongovernmental organizations: lessons for the UN. *Seton Hall Journal of Diplomacy and International Relations* Summer/Fall.

Gary Johns, 2014. *The Charity Ball: How to Dance to the Donors' Tune*. Melbourne: Connor Court.

Gary Johns, 2015. *No Contraception, No Dole: Tackling Intergenerational Welfare*. Brisbane: Connor Court.

Gary Johns, 2016. *Throw Open the Doors: the World Health Organization Framework Convention on Tobacco Control*. Brisbane: Connor Court.

L Joossens and M Raw, 2010. *The Tobacco Control Scale 2010 in Europe*. Association of European Cancer Leagues.

Ashley Kranjac and Robert Wagmiller, 2016. Decomposing trends in adult body mass index, obesity, and morbid obesity, 1971-2012. *Social Science and Medicine* 167.

Bjorn Larsen, 2016. Benefits and costs of household cooking options for air pollution control. *Copenhagen Consensus Center*, 26.

Paula Laws et al, 2006. Smoking and pregnancy. *Australian Institute of Health and Welfare, National Perinatal Statistics Unit* No. 33.

Pierre Lemieux, 2015. The dangers of 'public health'. *Regulation* Fall.

John Liberman, 2012. Four COPS and counting: achievements, under-achievements and looming challenges in the early life of the WHO FCTC Conference of the Parties. *Tobacco Control* 21(2).

A Lopez et al, 1994. A descriptive model of the cigarette epidemic in developed countries. *Tobacco Control* 3.

Melanie Lowe, 2014. Obesity and climate change mitigation in Australia: overview and analysis of policies with co-benefits. *Australian and New Zealand Journal of Public Health* 38(1).

Roger Magnusson, 2016. Is obesity a disease?: legal implications. *Obesity Australia Summit Papers*.

V.S. Malik et al, 2013. Global obesity: trends, risk factors and policy implications. *National Review of Endocrinology* 9(1).

Jerry Mander, 1978. *Four Arguments for the Elimination of Television*. New York: HarperCollins.

Sir Michael Marmot, Fair Australia: social justice and the health gap. *2016 Boyer Lectures* Australian Broadcasting Commission.

Marsden Jacob Associates, 2015. *Optimal Rates of Alcohol Taxation*.

Abraham Maslow, 1966. *The Psychology of Science*. Maurice Bassett Publishing.

Mario Mazzocchi and W. Bruce Traill, 2011. Calories, obesity and health in OECD countries. *Applied Economics* 43(26).

S W McCormack, 2010. Taking the good with the bad: recognizing the negative externalities created by charities and their implications for the charitable deduction. *Arizona Law Review* 52.

McKinsey Global Institute, 2014. Overcoming obesity: an initial economic analysis. *Discussion Paper*.

A McNeill, et al, 2012. Whither tobacco product regulation? *Tobacco Control* 21(2).

Zhen Miao et al, 2013. Accounting for product substitution in the analysis of food taxes targeting obesity. *Health Economics* 22.

Kathleen Michon, 2015. Tobacco litigation: history and recent developments. *NOLO* 30 December.

Rob Moodie et al, 2016. Australia's health: being accountable for prevention. *Medical Journal of Australia* 204(6).

John Morrison, 2014. *Social Licence: How To Keep Your Organisation Legitimate*. London: Palgrave Macmillan.

Scott Morrison, Treasurer of the Commonwealth of Australia. Second reading of the *Appropriation Bill (No. 1) 2016-17*. 3 May 2016.

Sendhil Mullainathan and Eldar Shafir. 2015. *Scarcity: The True Cost of Having Nothing*. Penguin (electronic).

Jill Nicholson-Crotty, 2011. Does reported policy activity reduce contributions to nonprofit service providers? *Policy Studies Journal* 39(4).

New South Wales Auditor-General's Report Performance Audit, 2013. *Cost of Alcohol Abuse to the NSW Government*.

New South Wales Office of Local Government, 2015. Swimming pool barrier requirements for backyard swimming pools in NSW. *Discussion Paper*.

D J Nutt et al, 2014. Estimating the harms of nicotine-containing products using the MCDA approach. *European Addiction Research* 20(2).

Obesity Australia 2013, *Action Agenda*.

Obesity Australia, 2015. *Rethink Obesity: A Media Guide on How to Report on Obesity*. Sydney.

Ombudsman New South Wales, Children Death Review Team, 2015. *Drowning Deaths of Children (Private Swimming Pools) 2007-2014*.

Adam Perkins, 2016. *The Welfare Trait: How State Benefits Affect Personality*. Palgrave Macmillan (electronic).

C Pisinger, 2014. Why public health people are more worried than excited over e-cigarettes. *BMC Medicine* 12.

Robert Proctor, 1999. *The Nazi War on Cancer*. New Jersey: Princeton University Press.

Public Health England, 2015. *E-Cigarettes: An Evidence Update*.

Price Waterhouse Coopers. 2015. *Weighing the Cost of Obesity: A Case for Action*.

R Room and K Mäkelä, 2000. Typologies of the cultural position of drinking. *Journal of the Study of Alcohol* 61(3).

Louise Russell, 2009. Preventing chronic disease: an important investment, but don't count on cost savings. *Health Affairs* 28(1).

Safe Work Australia, 2015. *Work-Related Traumatic Injury Fatalities, Australia 2014*.

L Shahab et al, 2017. Nicotine, carcinogen, and toxin exposure in long-term e-cigarette and nicotine replacement therapy users: A cross-sectional study. *Annals of Internal Medicine*, 7 February.

S Shulman, 2012. Establishing accountability for climate change damages: lessons from tobacco control. *Union of Concerned Scientists*.

Christopher Snowdon, 2015. Death and taxes: why living longer costs money. Institute for Economic Affairs, *Discussion Paper* no. 67.

K Stratton et al, 2001. Clearing the smoke: the science base for tobacco harm reduction. *Tobacco Control* 10(2).

St Vincent's Health Australia, 2016. *Restoring the Balance: A New Approach To Alcohol in Australia*. Melbourne: St. Vincent's Health Australia.

Norman Temple, 2012. Why prevention can increase health-care spending. *European Journal of Public Health* 22(5).

The Parliament of the Commonwealth of Australia, 2016. *Inquiry into the Register of Environmental Organisations House of Representatives Standing Committee on the Environment*.

The Parliament of the Commonwealth of Australia, *Charities Act 2013* (Cth).

The Parliament of the Commonwealth of Australia, *Corporations Act 2001* (Cth).

Matthew Thomas and Luke Buckmaster, 2010. Paternalism in social policy: when is it justifiable? *Australian Parliamentary Library Research Paper no. 8 2010-11*.

United States District Court for the District of Oregon. 2016. *Kelsey Cascade Rose Juliana et al versus The United States of America*. 6:15-cv-1517-TC.

United States District Court, Northern District of California (Oakland), *The Praxis Project v. The Coca-Cola Co.*, 17-cv-00016.

Lennert Veerman et al, 2016. The impact of a tax on sugar-sweetened beverages on health and health care costs: a modelling study. *PLOS ONE* 11(4).

Jamie Whyte, 2013. *Quack Policy Abusing Science in the Cause of Paternalism*. London: The Institute of Economic Affairs.

World Health Organization, 2003. *Technical Report Series. Diet, Nutrition and the Prevention of Chronic Diseases*.

World Health Organization, 2005. *WHO Framework Convention on Tobacco Control*.

World Health Organization Framework Convention on Tobacco Control, 2009. *History of the WHO Framework Convention on Tobacco Control*.

World Health Organization Framework Convention on Tobacco Control, 2014. *Reporting Instrument of The WHO Framework Convention On Tobacco Control* (Bangladesh).

World Health Organization Framework Convention on Tobacco Control, 2014. *Global Progress Report on the Implementation of the WHO Framework Convention on Tobacco Control*.

M Zeller and D Hatsukami, 2009. The strategic dialogue on tobacco harm reduction: a vision and blueprint for action in the US. *Tobacco Control* 18(4).

Index

www.ingramcontent.com/pod-product-compliance
Lightning Source LLC
Chambersburg PA
CBHW070407200326
41518CB00011B/2093